foundation guide
for
religious
grant seekers

2ND EDITION

SCHOLARS PRESS
HANDBOOK SERIES

Foundation Guide for Religious Grant Seekers
FRANCIS J. BUTLER & CATHERINE E. FARRELL
CO-EDITORS

Foundation Guide for Religious Grant Seekers

Francis J. Butler
&
Catherine E. Farrell
Co-Editors

SCHOLARS PRESS
CHICO, CALIFORNIA

Foundation Guide for Religious Grant Seekers
SECOND EDITION

Library of Congress Cataloging in Publication Data

Butler, Francis J.
    Foundation guide for religious grant seekers.

    (Scholars Press handbook series)
    Previous ed. by Peter S. Robinson
    Originally issued in series: Handbooks in humanities ;
no. 1.
    Bibliography: p.
    1. Church finance—Handbooks, manuals, etc. 2. Church
charities—Handbooks, manuals, etc. 3. Endowments—
United States—Directories. I. Farrell, Catherine E.
II. Robinson, Peter S.   Foundation guide for religious
grant seekers. III. Title. IV. Series.
BV774.5.B87   1984   262'.00681   84–10593
ISBN 0–89130–756–7 (pbk.)

Copyright © 1984
FADICA
Printed in the United States of America

Table of Contents

Acknowledgements

The Second Edition of the Foundation Guide for Religious Grantseekers was made possible through a grant provided by the Lilly Endowment. The Endowment, which has been an influential force in the enhancement of religious life in contemporary America, was instrumental in assisting FADICA in the preparation of the first edition of the Guide, published in 1979 under the editorship of Peter S. Robinson. The editors are grateful to the Endowment and in particular Dr. Robert Lynn for his encouragement in the updating of this publication.

Research for this current edition was undertaken with the help of the Foundation Center. The editors wish to express their sincere appreciation to Margot Brinkley, Director of the Washington, D.C., office of the Center, and to her staff who facilitated FADICA's efforts to revise the First Edition of the Guide.

Finally, the chief researcher of the project, Catherine E. Farrell, is to be acknowledged and heartily thanked for the many long hours which she devoted to reviewing the voluminous foundation records. Through Catherine Farrell's conscientious work the publishers are able to provide an excellent resource to lighten the task for the religious grantseeker.

Introduction

Although religion, as a category of "charitable" activity, accounts for nearly one-half of all private philanthropy in the United States, there are relatively few foundations active in the field of religion. The fact that private foundations with a genuine interest in religion are few and far between has made it difficult for religious organizations to know where to turn for help from foundations.

There has long been a need for a practical guide to help religious organizations (Catholic, Protestant and Jewish) locate foundations that might likely fund their projects or progams. With the exception of de Bettencourt's *The Catholic Guide to Foundations*, (Washington, D.C.: Guide Publishers, 1973), there has been no guide devoted solely to religious grant seeking until this one, which was first published in 1979. This second edition represents a number of changes and improvements over the first effort.

This, however, is not a "directory" of foundations interested in religion. A directory implies a comprehensive listing of foundations with detailed information about each. While this book does contain some minimal information about 384 foundations with a history of religious grant making, its basic function is to guide the reader to the right sources of information about these and other foundations so that he/she can undertake the necessary research to identify which ones, if any, would be interested in his/her proposal. The targeted approach is preferable (and more effective) in grant seeking than is the scattered approach. Too much precious time, money, and good will are lost through the indiscriminate barrage of proposals to foundations about which little or no research has been done. The chances of obtaining a grant improve in proportion to the research effort made to pinpoint those foundations with interests and priorities corresponding to the grant seeker's.

There is no way except through careful research to know which of the 22,000 grant-making foundations in the nation would be willing to fund a particular project. Foundations do not keep a list of grants available for the upcoming year. Instead, most foundations make broad statements of purpose such as "to aid social, educational, charitable, religious, or other organizations serving the common welfare." Proposals from grant seekers are considered at board meetings of the foundations and funding decisions are made. Time should be taken to investigate thoroughly the foundations to which proposals are sent. An important point in grant searching is the assurance that the foundation is interested in a specific field of endeavor.

This guide will enable seekers to locate compatible foundations.

This book also intends to help answer the question: Is a foundation grant really what is needed or wanted? Not only is a foundation grant hard to get but it can, in some cases, be counter-productive. What may be needed might not be foundation support, but better support from an organization's own constituency since its long-term financial well being lies there, not with foundations. To the extent that the prospect of foundation support distracts one from that realization, genuine harm is done.

Finally, the guide may help an applicant realize that foundations have a rather limited place and role in private philanthropy in general and in religious philanthropy in particular. The guide, therefore, presents a four-point plan to aid in building one's own constituency.

Section I

SOURCES OF INFORMATION AVAILABLE ON FOUNDATIONS

The Foundation Center

The Foundation Center is the only nonprofit organization which exists solely to gather, analyze, and disseminate information on American private foundations and their grants. It was established by foundations to provide information for the grant-seeking public and is largely maintained by contributions from foundations. The Center provides (1) free library service to the walk-in public and (2) invaluable publications with information on philanthropic giving and how to determine where to apply most appropriately for funding. (See below for description of these publications.) The Center operates libraries in New York, Washington, Cleveland, and San Francisco. In addition, it supplies publications and other resources to cooperating collections in over 75 public, university, government, and foundation libraries in 50 states, Mexico, and Puerto Rico. (See *Appendix A* for locations of these libraries.) The Center provides the following services at its national collections:

- Reference librarians to help visitors use resource materials
- Free weekly orientations; call for reservations
- Special orientations arranged for groups, classes, or meetings
- Microform and paper copying facilities
- Associates Program—fee service for those needing frequent and immediate access to foundation information.

The cooperating libraries throughout the nation house regional collections. They contain all of the Center's reference works, recent books, and information on foundations, foundation annual reports, and IRS returns pertinent to those foundations within their state or region. Many have staff members who will assist the grant seeker not only in using the local resources but also by contacting the Center's national libraries for more detailed information.

The Publications of the Foundation Center

Copies of the Center's publications are available for free reference use in all of the libraries, and some may be available in other local, public, and university libraries. The following publications may be purchased by writing the Center.

1

(1) Directories Describing Foundations

Foundation Directory. Includes entries arranged alphabetically within states for approximately 4,000 of the largest foundations. Contains most of the following information: name, address, statement of purpose and interest, officers, financial data, some phone numbers, and some grant application guidelines. (For the latest edition, call Toll Free 800-424-9836)

Source Book Profiles. Annual loose-leaf service with in-depth analyses of programs of 1000 major foundations making annual grants of $200,000 or more per year. The top thousand foundations are profiled on a two-year cycle with 500 new profiles issued per year and over 80 new foundations profiled every other month. Updates are issued when personnel, address, program, etc., changes occur at any foundation profiled to date.

National Data Book. Includes brief entries for over 22,000 foundations. Volume I is arranged alphabetically by name; Volume II contains a complete list of the foundations within each state in descending order of grant amounts. Used together, volumes provide complete address, contact person, and financial information on virtually all active foundations in the United States regardless of size.

Foundation Grants to Individuals. Describes programs of nine hundred and fifty foundations which make grants to individuals. Subject index includes Religion, Religious Studies, Rabbinical Studies, Religious Leadership, and other appropriate subjects for the religious grant seeker.

(2) Indexes to Foundation Grants

Foundation Grants Index. Annual volume which incorporates grants of $5,000 or more of about three hundred and sixty major foundations.

COMSEARCH Printouts. Computer printouts listing grants and foundations making the grants in particular subject areas (See printouts on RELIGION #110 and RELIGIOUS EDUCATION #111.) Custom computer searches done on more specific topics for foundations and for subscribers to the Center's Associates Program. Searches on The Foundation Grants Index, Foundation Directory.

(3) Guides for Grant Seekers

About Foundations. A guide to funding research
What Will a Foundation Look for When You Submit a Grant Proposal?
What Makes A Good Proposal?

Internal Revenue Service Form (990-PF)

If a foundation qualifies as private, it is required to file a 990-Private Foundation Form which then become available to the public on the microfiche cards. The following information is found on the forms/cards:

- Name and address of the foundation
- Total assets for the year at market and book value

- Telephone numbers (sometimes just the foundation's accountant)
- Total contributions, gifts, and grants received
- List of the contributions, gifts, and grants paid during the year
- Principal officers, directors, and trustees
- Detailed financial information

The list of grants paid is particularly useful to the grant seeker because it contains the recipients and amounts. The IRS forms are invaluable because for many of the smaller foundations they are the only source of detailed information; only the larger foundations publish printed annual reports and qualify for directories. The IRS forms are recorded on microfiche cards and complete sets on every foundation can be obtained at the Foundation Center in New York City and Washington, D.C. or from the Internal Revenue Service. Each regional collection has a full set of these cards for the foundations located in its state or region. By the fall of each year, the file should be largely complete for the preceding year. Staff are available at the Center's libraries to assist you in your research with these IRS forms.

Completed IRS forms also put the foundations' giving patterns in perspective. The grant seeker may find a foundation described in the *Foundation Directory* as being interested in "church support," "religious associations," or "religious purposes," only to find in the IRS form that its support in the religious field was miniscule in comparison to the foundations' funding of other fields of interest.

Annual Reports Published by the Foundations

Only about 500 foundations publish and distribute annual reports which serve to inform the public about their activities. Such publications are generally valuable sources of information, containing lists of grants paid and grants committed to future payment, definitions of program interests, names of officers, and detailed financial statements. For the religious grant seeker, the self-description of the areas of funding interest and the lists of grants paid are useful for pointing out the extent of the foundations's interest in religion.

To find out if a foundation publishes a report, consult the *Foundation Directory.* Most of the foundations that publish annual reports are among the 4,063 major foundations listed in edition 9 of the Directory, and the words "report published annually" at the end of the paragraph describing the purpose and activities of the foundation will indicate which they are.

Another place to find out if a particular foundation publishes an annual report is the *Foundation Center National Data Book* available for use at the Foundation Center's national and regional libraries. This two volume publication previously mentioned as listing over 21,000 currently active grant-making foundations marks with an asterisk those foundations publishing annual reports. Most foundations publishing annual reports

3

print enough copies to fill public requests. The Foundation Center's national and regional libraries also have copies of these reports.

State Directories of Foundations

Approximately forty states have directories listing or describing the foundations within their regional or state boundaries. These guides are important sources of information as many foundations award grants only in their locale. These state directories are available at Foundation Center libraries and at some public and university libraries. See *Appendix B* for a bibliography of state foundation directories.

Other Sources of Information

The Catholic Guide to Foundations. Edition 2 (1973). Francis de Bettencourt, P. O. Box 5849, Washington, DC 20014. Guide Publishers, Washington, DC. An alphabetical list of 336 foundations in 48 states with information derived from IRS reports. Because it is very dated, this guide should be used in conjunction with the other source material, especially the latest edition of the *Foundation Directory*, the IRS 990 returns on microfiche, or the state directories to update the information shown. In many cases, foundations listed have ceased to exist.

Foundation Reporter. Taft Corporation. 1000 Vermont Ave., N.W., Washington, DC 20005. Includes 500 major American foundations, board members described, lists of grants paid, and description of purposes. There are nine regional publications and one national publication, updated annually.

Foundation 500. Douglas M. Lawson Association, 39 East 51st Street, New York, NY 10022. Categorizes 500 largest foundations by general subject areas, amount of giving and giving patterns. (Updated yearly).

The Grantmanship Center News. Six issues annually. Grantmanship Center, 1015 West Olympic Blvd., Los Angeles, CA 90015. Magazine format. Keeps extremely up-to-date with items, articles, features on all forms of fund raising.

Annual Register of Grant Support. Marquis Who's Who, 4300 West 62nd Street, Indianapolis, IN 46206. Updated annually. Lists grant programs supported by foundations, government agencies, corporations, etc. Only directory that covers both public and private funding sources.

Where America's Large Foundations Make Their Grants. Public Service Materials Center, 355 Lexington Avenue, New York, NY 10017. Edited by Joseph Dermer. (Updated yearly).

Catalog of Federal Domestic Assistance. Executive Office of the President (OMB), Washington, DC 20503. For sale by Supt. of Documents, U.S. Government Printing Office, Washington, DC 20402. Marvellously indexed, kept up-to-date by loose-leaf additions throughout the year.

4

(This book is helpful to those religious organizations seeking public funding for educational and/or social service purposes).

COMSEARCH *Printouts.* Foundation Center (Call Toll Free 800-424-9836). Computer produced subject guides to recent foundation grants. An easy to use listing of grants under 114 categories. (Updated annually).

Section II
THE GRANT SEEKING PROCESS

Now that the resource materials have been identified you may be asking, "But how do I actually begin my search for a foundation that makes grants for religious activities?" The following steps and questions should help you get started.

(1) Use the Foundation Center library system. If you cannot travel to one of the national libraries, check you regional collection. Do not hesitate to ask the staff for help. This alone will help you avoid many problems and wrong turns.

(2) Identify foundations with a *possible* interest in your project by using the list in this guide and the directories and indexes described above.

(3) Research *each* of these foundations for answers to the following questions:

   (a) What is the extent of the foundation's religious funding? Examine the IRS forms or the annual reports for the list of grants paid. Look to see what percentage of grants went to religion. Also check on what type of organizations received grants.

   (b) Does the foundation have geographic limitations on its grant making? Look to see if grants were made only in the foundation's locale or on a national or international basis. It is very important to know if a foundation only funds projects in its region. The directories and annual reports contain this information. As a rule, the likelihood of getting a grant from a foundation diminishes with distance. Therefore, be sure you know all of the possibilities in your locale.

   (c) Does the foundation have financial ability to respond to your request? Check the assets and size of the average grant paid out.

   (d) Does the foundation have any specific limitations or conditions on its grant awarding? Check for guidelines on what type of grants will or will not be made. For example, some foundations will not make grants to individuals, nor will they support building funds. These special limitations will be found in the directories describing the foundations.

   (e) Does the foundation publish procedures by which to apply for a grant? Check the directories and annual reports for any possible deadline for submitting proposals and for the schedule of board meetings.

(4) Once you have done the appropriate research on the foundations you plan to approach, you are ready to make the initial contact. This initial contact can be by either telephone or letter to briefly describe your program and needs and to ask if the foundation would be interested in receiving a proposal. If there is interest, ask for information concerning the correct procedure, the time for applying, and the possibility of a personal interview. (Often the most effective way to get a grant is through a person-to-person interview.) Contact should first be made with the appropriate person on the foundation's staff. If there is no staff, find the person who has been designated to be contacted. He/she will likely be an officer or trustee. If there is a staff, do not attempt to approach a trustee without the staff's knowing it. This would be not only poor etiquette, but also a ploy that can easily work to your detriment.

(5) The best guidelines in writing a proposal are the ones the foundation itself may provide you. If no guidelines are provided, it is up to you to state your cause as best you can in a format that seems most appropriate to your situation. Be accurate in what is said and avoid grandiose language. Make it evident that you are aware of what has been and is being done by others relative to the needs or concerns to which your proposal is addresed. Proposal writing is largely a matter of common sense and clear narrative writing. The following are certain basic elements that all proposals ought to contain.

(a) Statements of:
- Nature and purpose of your organization. (By way of introduction.)
- The problem or need.
- What you propose to do about it. (Objectives and methods of action.)
- What makes your proposal or approach distinctive from comparable requests from other institutions.
- The anticipated outcome. (What, when, and ways of measuring success.)
- Who is involved in the program and what are their qualifications. (Only cite credentials pertinent to the effort to be undertaken.)
- Expected grant period. (Have you taken into account the amount of time the foundation will need to make its decision?)
- How the proposed program relates to other institutions and resources pertinent to the need described.
- Endorsements or references. (Any enclosed letters of endorsement ought to illumine the particular qualifications of the persons involved in the program and not deal with extraneous qualities.)

(b) Financial information about:
  - The budget and overall financial context of the plan.
  - The amount of grant support being requested.
  - Other sources of support.
  - Provision for on-going support of the program. (Vague assurances are not reassuring.)
  - Evidence of tax-exemption.

(c) Summary

The highlights of the proposal ought to be summarized on one or two pages and put at the beginning along with a letter of transmittal.

Several publications designed to help the proposal writer are available through the Foundation Center and may be obtained by writing the New York office or by visiting one of their libraries.

A final reminder is in order about the importance of thoroughly researching the foundations to which you send proposals. No matter what amount of effort is put into it, your proposal will prove worthless if it is sent to foundations which have no interest in your area of concern.

Section III

THE VIEW FROM THE OTHER SIDE OF THE DESK

Foundations, and organizations which seek grants from them, have a common allegiance: both are members of what is increasingly known as the "third sector"—the world of non-profit, private "voluntary" agencies and organizations. The other two sectors are, of course, business and government. All three provide either goods or services, but with significantly different imperatives and motives. Each is integral to American society and our system of checks and balances.

Three significant characteristics of American society largely account for the existence of the third sector: (1) the American impulse to altruism, voluntary giving of money, time and other private resources to meet the needs of others; (2) our penchant to organize ourselves into private, voluntary efforts in order to apply those resources systematically to social problem solving; and (3) our long tradition of pluralism and cultural diversity. Each of these traits also serves to explain the almost uniquely American phenomenon of private foundations.

Although private foundations fully share in the origin and experience of charitable organizations, in whatever field of endeavor—education, social welfare, the arts and sciences, conservation, religion, etc.—there is still a great deal of misunderstanding about their nature and role, particularly on the part of the grant seeker.

It is hard for grant seekers to put themselves into the position of the foundation representative. Part of this difficulty is due to the failure of the foundations themselves. By and large foundations have been reticent about explaining their problems and aspirations to the public, sometimes because of a sense of humility consistent with Scriptural injunctions against the dangers of advertising one's own good deeds. More often, however, foundations are reluctant to be too visible lest their explanations about themselves invite an avalanche of requests.

Perhaps the root of the problem lies even deeper. There is almost unavoidable distance between the grant maker and the grant seeker. From the point of view of the aspiring grantee, the foundation often appears to enjoy ample resources or at least enough money to make "just this one grant." Yet, that is not how it looks from the other side of the desk. The foundation official, whether a trustee or staff member, is apt to be aware of a different kind of abundance, namely, the sheer plenitude of significant opportunities for grant making and the relative scarcity of foundation

11

funds to meet even a fraction of these possibilities. Where one sees abundance the other sees scarcity.

This gap between abundance of opportunities and scarcity of available resources necessarily affects the ways in which even the most affluent foundations go about their work. While foundations react to this pressure in different ways, there are at least two contrasting tendencies in their responses.

1) In view of the scarcity of foundation funds and the consequently increased importance of these resources, many foundations prefer to stay with the "tried and true" causes. If a foundation leans in this direction, then it will be more likely to favor support of already existing institutions and to be willing to provide a subsidy for on-going programs or perhaps for "brick and mortar" needs. The foundation, in effect, takes its place alongside of the individual donor and makes a contribution to maintain or improve the *status quo*. Such a donation seldom represents a risk or causes controversy, except, perhaps, from those who were disappointed that this program subsidy did not go to their organization.

2) The opposing tendency leads to a quite different response. In the judgement of some foundation representatives, the preoccupation of supporting the proven institutions and programs deflects foundations from making their most distinctive contributions. At its best American philanthropy has constituted an early warning system about the problems and possibilities that lie ahead in the future. A good grant has been one that has helped illumine the landscape of tomorrow: the needs of our society, what changes are now necessary to prepare ourselves for them, and what pitfalls to avoid as we move into the future.

Philanthropists who accept this view of foundation grant-making recognize a distinction between the role and capacities foundations can assume in our society and the role the individual donor plays.

All positive change involves risk. Foundations, unlike most donors, are uniquely prepared to assume risks in the interests of society. Their distributable funds can be "invested" in imaginative programs and projects whose chances of success are tentative and whose ability to make a "return" (least of all to the foundation) is not important. In very many such cases foundations represent the only feasible source of financial support. Foundations can also afford to live with an unpopular line of inquiry without having to worry unduly about an anxious public. These institutions can stay with issues long enough to weigh the long-term effects or to seek out alternative solutions because they can, if they will, resist the temptation to join the passing parade of fads and fancies.

Such an exploration of the future is not, of course, without its hazards. Foundations can—and do!—guess wrongly about significant issues. It is all the more important, therefore, that foundations have the freedom to admit their errors and thereby to gain the confidence and support of the community at large by searching out the most important problems of the coming years.

The role of the individual donor in private philanthropy contrasts significantly with that of foundations. It would not be overstating the matter to say that the survival of voluntary organizations depends on the continued altruism of the individual donor and not on foundations. The free will contributions of money and service by individual donors are what most private charitable organizations rely on to close the gap between operating income and actual costs. In short, the indispensable role of the individual donor in private philanthropy is subsidizing charitable institutions. The statistics bear this out.

To begin with there are only about 22,000 private grant-making foundations in the United States, and all but about 3,000 are extremely small (with less than one million dollars each in assets). On the other hand, the number of individual donors is legion, comprising practically the whole of the adult community to some degree. (The word "donor" might be misleading in its connotation since what is being referred to is the small contributor as well as the large).

In 1982, individual donors in the United States provided $48.69 billion, or 89.7 percent, of all private philanthropy.* This figure does not include another $5.45 billion in bequests nor does it include the billions of hours of contributed service time. Corporations and businesses contributed $3.10 billion and foundations another $3.15 billion. Altogether, private philanthropy in the United States totalled $60.39 billion that year, only 5.2 percent of which came from foundations.

In the field of religion, the percentage contrast of total contributions made by foundations versus individuals becomes even more extreme. Less than two percent of the $28.06 billion of private philanthropy that was directed to the field of religion during 1982 came from foundations. Almost without exception, the rest came from individual donors and accounted for nearly half (46%) of all private giving to charity of any variety!

What can be inferred from these figures in forming a realistic attitude toward foundations and private philanthropy in general when seeking financial support for religious organizations?

For one thing, we can gain a better sense of realism about the limitations of foundations as sources of financial support to religious organizations. The total amount of funds available to religious activities from foundations is infinitesimal compared to the funds contributed by individuals. There are precious few foundations active in the field of religion. In the course of preparing this guide, the authors were able to identify about 384 such foundations from the approximately 4,000 largest throughout the country, and most of these are local in their giving preferences. Moreover, the volume of requests these foundations typically receive far exceeds their available funds. In general, therefore, the chances of getting a grant from a founda-

*All figures are taken from the 1983 Annual Report of the American Association of Fund Raising Counsel, Inc. entitled *Giving USA*.

13

tion are slim and become narrower the greater the distance separating the foundation from the organization applying for a grant. It is therefore very important to target one's grant request as precisely as possible through careful research in identifying those foundations most likely to be able and willing to respond positively.

Second, one ought to respect the fact that foundations are a scarce source of risk capital for program areas where change and development are needed and where there is no other source of support. There are few other comparable sources of this "venture capital" available to the voluntary sector. Foundations, therefore, should not be asked to replace the private donor in subsidizing the operating and normal program expenses of charitable organizations, nor to aid projects whose support could come from the organization's own constituency if an adequate effort were only made. Such grants would amount to a misuse of a very limited and valuable resource for both the society and for religion in particular.

Third, it is unwise automatically to look to foundations as a solution to the financial needs or problems of your organization or program. The very existence of foundations—all that free money— engenders in too many charitable and religious organizations a reflexive reaction to turn to them, the foundations, for help. In this connection, it can be parenthetically noted that grant seekers often turn to private foundations without considering the resources available for charitable purposes within grant-making religious bodies. Nearly every major denomination maintains a funding entity of some type. Many of them are significantly larger than the typical private foundation.

The prospect of foundation aid can serve to harm charitable organizations if allowed to distract them from the realization that their long term survival and well-being depends on receiving aid from their own support community. Rarely can foundations be found to be a direct part of the constituency of any one charitable or religious organization. It is a major, and sometimes fatal, error for charities to perceive foundations as such.

The fact is that the future of voluntary organizations and institutions depends almost entirely upon the extent to which they are able to develop a strong and lasting financial base from a compassionate support community. This means recognizing potential members of this community, nurturing them, and actively involving them in the life of the organization and its programs. Thus if, in responding to the imperative of raising more funds, you find yourself spending most of your time and energy trying to interest foundations in your program needs and not trying to develop your own support community, you are probably doing everybody, including yourself, a disservice. To better understand how a voluntary organization can develop a lasting financial base, the following section is provided.

Section IV
BUILDING CONSTITUENCY SUPPORT

A voluntary organization is wise to seek a broad base of support. Dependency on a single source of support, no matter how adequate and comfortable it may be for the time being, is almost certain to lead to severe financial problems in the future, probably the near future. Typically, a broad base of support for a volunteer organization would include all or most of the following:

(1) Fees for service, tuition, or membership
(2) Endowment income
(3) Contributions
(4) Revenue from federal, state, or local government agencies
(5) Sale of publications
(6) Auxiliary enterprises (housing and food services)

No matter what percent of the annual budget is derived from contributions, it is desirable to obtain gifts from a variety of sources. Here again, dependency on a single source, or a very small number of donors, places an organization in a high-risk position. Individuals may die, change their interests, or even become disenchanted with the organization. Foundations rarely provide extended funding. Corporations tie their giving to profits which usually fluctuate from year to year, and they generally like to spread their contributions over a rather large number of recipients. In addition, very few foundations or corporations will give to organizations which have a specific religious orientation.

Four Characteristics of Successful Fund Raising

Financial stability for most voluntary organizations requires that the fund raising effort be successful. Success means that annual objectives for number of donors and dollars are met. There are four characteristics of successful fund raising which are quite prominent. These will not exist to the same degree with all groups, and a single organization which is successful in fund raising may see some variations in these characteristics from year to year.

(1) Program Worthy of Support

The first characteristic of a successful fund raising effort is that the organization maintains a program of service which is worthy of support. It has a reputation for doing well what it purports to do. Those who know about the organization, if only slightly, believe it is doing something worthwhile. The extent to which an organization is known and truly understood will vary greatly. Some are much more adept than others in publicizing their activities. The point is, when an organization is successful in raising funds, it will be providing a service or program which any fairminded person who came in contact with it would agree to its deserving support.

(2) Constituency with Ability to Provide Support

The second characteristic of a successful fund raising effort is a constituency which has the financial ability to provide the required support. This may be a natural constituency or a developed constituency. Examples of a natural constituency would be alumni of an educational institution, former patients of a hospital, season members of a symphony orchestra, or parishioners of a church. A developed constituency would include individuals, corporations, and organizations which have been made aware of the voluntary organization's program and have shown a willingness to help support it. They may or may not become directly involved with the program or service of the charitable organization.

In attempting to establish a developed constituency, it is important to identify those who truly have the financial potential for providing support. Many organizations tend to look far and wide for prospects, when their best potentials may be within a few blocks or miles of the institution. As a matter of fact, most organizations which are successful in fund raising receive significant gift dollars from board and staff members before seeking outside support.

Regular and systematic approaches need to be made to the constituents to keep them informed. It is hazardous to assume that even those who are fairly close to the work of an organization are fully aware of the program and financial situation. Newsletters, brochures, audio visuals, and on-location visits will help interpret the organization to its natural and developed constituents.

(3) Fund Raising Plan

The third characteristic of an organization which is successful in obtaining gift support is that it has a plan for fund raising. The plan may be a few pages in length or it may be a large and greatly detailed document. Size is not important. What is essential is that the effort be given careful thought and that it represents the commitment of the fund raising staff, the chief executive, the administrative staff, and the board of directors. Some of the elements in a typical fund raising plan will include:

(a) Statement of organizational objectives.
(b) Narrative which justifies gift support.

(c) Detailed financial goal(s).

(d) Time schedule for each phase of the fund raising effort.

(e) Budget for fund raising program.

(f) Decision regarding personal solicitation, telephone solicitation, direct mail, benefit or special event, sale of merchandise.

(g) Determining type of gift sought—outright, gifts with reservation of life income, or bequests.

(h) Decision whether gift principal or income only is to be used.

(i) Establishing method of receiving gifts, gift acknowledgements, gift accounting.

(4) Leadership for Fund Raising.

The final characteristic of an effort which is successful in fund raising is that there are leaders who are able to implement the fund raising plan. Most experienced development officers would agree that this is the most important of the four characteristics cited. Why is leadership for fund raising so important? It is rather well accepted that people give to people. The personal relationship that exists between solicitor and donor will usually be the determining factor.

Leadership for fund raising divides into two categories, staff leadership and volunteer leadership. Both are critical if the organization hopes to obtain maximum results. Staff leadership for fund raising begins with the chief executive. This person must give it a high priority even though he may spend a relatively low percent of his time in fund raising. Operating responsibility for fund raising rests with the development officer. This person must coordinate the fund raising activities of the chief executive and other staff members and the volunteer fund raisers. The volunteer leadership for fund raising usually begins with the board of directors. There may also be an advisory board or a development committee which takes primary responsibility.

Whatever the structure, organizations that achieve well in gift support have volunteers who are effective in giving and getting gifts. Conversely, most fund raising failures can be traced to a lack of leadership for fund raising. Experience shows that an organization will be successful in raising funds if it has a program worthy of support, identifies or develops a constituency with ability to give, prepares a plan for fund raising, and then enlists leaders to carry out the plan.

17

Section V

FOUNDATIONS WITH PAST INTEREST IN FUNDING RELIGIOUS ORGANIZATIONS

The following list of foundations with a history of funding religious activities is not to be considered all-inclusive. It was largely compiled from the most recent IRS returns of each foundation. These were examined in the fall of 1983 to determine the actual extent of its grant making in the field of religion. The principal researcher reviewed the entries in the first edition of the *Foundation Guide* and found by checking the federal returns that ninety-nine of the previous 322 entries of the first edition of the Foundation Guide had to be eliminated for failing to meet the following criteria: (1) made grants to more than one religious organization (unless an unusually large amount), (2) total grants to religion were either $25,000 annually or a sizeable percent of the foundation's annual giving, and (3) grants were for religious purposes specifically and not for religious-sponsored organizations such as schools and welfare groups. However, using new information gathered from COMSEARCH printouts and the 9th edition of the *Foundation Directory* as verified by a review of IRS returns, an additional 161 new entries were made to the present edition.

The result is this list, which includes the largest foundations in the nation with an interest in religion, as well as some smaller foundations with almost exclusive interest in religion. The foundations fall into three broad categories (and some overlap into more than one of these divisions):

(1) Foundations almost solely devoted to religious funding.

(2) Large foundations with a sizeable amount of funding in the religious area, although religion is only one area of interest.

(3) Foundations which fund religious activities only in their locale or as a secondary area of funding interest.

This list does not include many foundations which give grant money to religious organizations for education, health, social welfare, or other "secular" programs. Those religious institutions seeking grant support for such programs are advised to consult the subject index of the latest edition of the *Foundation Directory*, the subject index of the *Foundation Center Source Book Profiles*, the appropriate COMSEARCH printout, and other reference sources found at the Foundation Center libraries and cooperating libraries identified in this guide.

The list also may not include the names of many small foundations

19

which support religious activities in their own locale. These may be found in the various state directories.

Warning! Take this list for what it is—a compilation of the foundations with a past history of funding religious organizations. It should be a time-saver as it gives the grant seeker a starting place when searching for religious grants from among the 22,000 foundations. However, remember to do further research on the foundations that might fund your project. You cannot be sure until you do your homework.

Protestant Foundations

Alabama

CHRISTIAN WORKERS FOUNDATION, THE
3577 Bankhead Avenue
Montgomery, AL 36111
Contact Person: Allen W. Mathis, Jr., Director
Geographic Giving Pattern: National
Special Interest: Evangelical organizations

Mc WANE FOUNDATION
P.O. Box 43327
Birmingham, AL 35243
Contact Person: J.R. McWane
Geographic Giving Pattern: Local
Special Interest: Education, Protestant church support

MITCHELL FOUNDATION, INC., THE
2405 First National Bank Building
P.O. Box 1126
Mobile, AL 36601
(205) 432-1711
Contact Person: M.L. Screven, Jr., Secretary
Geographic Giving Pattern: Primarily local
Special Interest: Religious welfare agencies,
   Protestant church support

SMITH (THE M.W.) JR. FOUNDATION
P.O. Box 691
Daphne, AL 36526
(205) 626-5436
Contact Person: Mary M. Riser, Secretary
Geographic Giving Pattern: Primarily S.W. Alabama
Special Interest: Protestant religious welfare programs and churches

Alaska

KAELBER PRIVATE FOUNDATION
3808 Locarno Drive
Anchorage, AK 99504
(907) 276-5716

Contact Person: Norman F. Kaelber
Special Interest: Higher education, Protestant churches

RASMUSSON FOUNDATION
c/o National Bank of Alaska, Trustee
Box 600
Anchorage, AK 99510
(907) 265-2959

Contact Person: National Bank of Alaska
Geographic Giving Pattern: Local
Special Interest: Higher education, Christian churches

Arizona

GOPPERT FOUNDATION, THE
8336 Calle de Alegria
Scottsdale, AZ 85255
(602) 858-7043

Contact Person: Howard E. Bunton, Vice-President
Geographic Giving Pattern: Primarily local
Special Interest: Higher education, hospitals, church support

TELL FOUNDATION, THE
20 Biltmore Estates
Phoenix, AZ 85016

Contact Person: Andrew P. Tell, President
Geographic Giving Pattern: Primarily local
Special Interest: To support Protestant churches and church related
institutions

Arkansas

JONES (THE HARVEY AND BERNICE) FOUNDATION
P.O. Box 233
Springdale, AR 72764
(501) 751-2730

Contact Person: Harvey Jones, Chairman
Geographic Giving Pattern: Primarily local
Special Interest: Protestant churches and church organizations

21

MURPHY FOUNDATION, THE
Murphy Building
El Dorado, AR 71730
(501) 862-6411

Contact Person: Lucy A. Ring, Secretary
Geographic Giving Pattern: Primarily local
Special Interest: Higher education - scholarships, Protestant church
   support and youth agencies

REBSAMEN FUND
P.O. Box 3198
Little Rock, AR 72203
(501) 661-4800

Contact Person: Doris B. Bowling, Treasurer
Geographic Giving Pattern: Primarily local
Special Interest: Recreation and civic also religious

RIGGS BENEVOLENT FUND
c/o Worthen Bank and Trust Company
P.O. Box 1681
Little Rock, AR 72203
(501) 378-1237

Contact Person: Worthen Bank and Trust
Geographic Giving Pattern: Primarily local
Special Interest: Higher education, Protestant church support and
   church related organizations

STURGIS (THE ROY AND CHRISTINE) CHARITABLE AND EDUCATIONAL TRUST
P.O. Box 92
Malvern, AR 72104
(501) 332-3506

Contact Person: Katie Speer, Trustee
Geographic Giving Pattern: Primarily local
Special Interest: Protestant church support, hospitals, youth and
   social agencies, education

California

AHMANSON FOUNDATION, THE
3731 Wilshire Boulevard
Los Angeles, CA 90010
(213) 383-1381

Contact Person: Kathleen A. Gilcrest, Vice-President and Secretary
Geographic Giving Pattern: Largely local
Special Interest: Broad - emphasis on education, arts and
humanities, medicine and health and religious organizations

ARTEVEL FOUNDATION
c/o Security Pacific Plaza
333 S. Hope St., Suite 3710
Los Angeles, CA 90071

Contact Person: George R. Phillips, Secretary-Treasurer
Geographic Giving Pattern: National, international
Special Interest: Protestant evangelical and missionary programs

ATKINSON FOUNDATION
10 W. Orange Avenue S
S. San Francisco, CA 94080
(415) 876-1559

Contact Person: Donald K. Grant, Treasurer
Geographic Giving Pattern: Northern California and overseas
Special Interest: Methodist church, divisions of World Missions also
    activities of Willamette University

ATKINSON (MYRTLE L.) FOUNDATION
c/o Mrs. Elizabeth A. Whitsett
P.O. Box 688
La Canada, CA 91011
(213) 790-7029

Contact Person: Mrs. Elizabeth A. Whitsett, President
Geographic Giving Pattern: National, international
Special Interest: Evangelical church unity. Also to "encourage and
    promote religious, scientific, technical and all other kinds of
    education, enlightenment and research"

BERRY (THE LOWELL) FOUNDATION
One Kaiser Plaza, Suite 890
Oakland, CA 94612
(415) 452-0433

Contact Person: Charles Branagh, President
Geographic Giving Pattern: Alameda/Contra Costa area
Special Interest: Evangelical Protestant church-related programs and
    institutions

BULL (THE HENRY W.) FOUNDATION
c/o Wells Fargo Bank
420 Montgomery No. 954
San Francisco, CA 94163
(415) 396-3105

Contact Person: James W.Z. Taylor, Administrator
Geographic Giving Pattern: Primarily local
Special Interest: Higher education, handicapped, church support

CADDOCK FOUNDATION, INC.
640 Sandalwood Court
Riverside, CA 92507
(714) 684-6326

Contact Person: Richard E. Caddock, President
Geographic Giving Pattern: Primarily local
Special Interest: Protestant religious associations, Bible studies

COBURN (THE MAURINE CHURCH) CHARITABLE TRUST
c/o Wells Fargo Bank, Trust Department
P.O. Box 2229
Monterey, CA 93940

Contact Person: Milton C. Coburn, Trustee
Geographic Giving Pattern: Primarily local
Special Interest: Protestant church related institutions

CRUMMEY (VIVIAN G.) BENEVOLENT TRUST
1441 University Avenue
San Jose, CA 95126
(408) 296-6585

Contact Person: Carolyn H. Crummey, Trustee
Geographic Giving Pattern: Primarily local
Special Interest: United Methodist churches, theological education,
  missionary programs

FOREST LAWN FOUNDATION
1712 So. Glendale Avenue
Glendale, CA 91205
(213) 254-3131

Contact Person: John Llewellyn, Vice-President
Geographic Giving Pattern: Primarily local
Special Interest: Religious institutions, higher education, health and
  welfare, hospitals

GILMORE (EARL B.) FOUNDATION
6301 W. Third Street
P.O. Box 480314
Los Angeles, CA 90048
(213) 939-1191

Contact Person: M.B. Hartman, Treasurer
Geographic Giving Pattern: Primarily local
Special Interest: Protestant church support, higher and secondary education, health and youth agencies, hospitals

GOSPEL FOUNDATION OF CALIFORNIA
1462 North Stanley Avenue
Hollywood, CA 90046
(213) 876-2172

Contact Person: Mary E. Liddecoat, President
Geographic Giving Pattern: Primarily in California
Special Interest: Christian religious, charitable, educational, evangelistic and mission enterprises

GREENVILLE FOUNDATION, THE
P.O. Box 885
Pacific Palisades, CA 90272

Contact Person: Wm. Miles, Jr., Chairman
Special Interest: Protestant religious programs and higher education including a school of theology

HELMS FOUNDATION, INC.
P.O. Box 312
Redwood Valley, CA 95470

Contact Person: W.D. Manuel, Assistant Secretary
Geographic Giving Pattern: Primarily local
Special Interest: Protestant church support and religious education

JAMESON (J.W. AND IDA M.) FOUNDATION
P.O. Box 397
Sierra Madre, CA 91024
(213) 355-9673

Contact Person: Arthur W. Kirk, President
Geographic Giving Pattern: Primarily in California
Special Interest: Higher education including theological seminaries. Also for Protestant church support

LAYNE FOUNDATION
19 Rue Cannes
Newport Beach, CA 92660
(714) 644-4059

Contact Person: Robert H. Mason, President
Geographic Giving Pattern: Southern California
Special Interest: Low-interest loans to Christian churches and religious organizations

LLOYD (THE RALPH B.) FOUNDATION
9441 Olympic Blvd.
Beverly Hills, CA 90212

Contact Person: Mrs. Eleanor Dees, President
Geographic Giving Pattern: Primarily in California and Oregon
Special Interest: Protestant church support, education

MUNGER (ALFRED C.) FOUNDATION
c/o Richard D. Esbenshade
612 So. Flower Street, 5th floor
Los Angeles, CA 90017
(213) 624-7715

Contact Person: Charles T. Munger
Geographic Giving Pattern: Primarily local
Special Interest: Protestant religious organizations

MURDY FOUNDATION
1633 E. Fourth Street, Suite 156
Santa Ana, CA 92701
(714) 543-2849

Contact Person: John A. Murdy, Jr.
Geographic Giving Pattern: Primarily local
Special Interest: Higher education, Protestant church support,
   cultural programs

ORLETON TRUST FUND
1777 Borel Place, Suite 306
San Mateo, CA 94402
(415) 345-2818

Contact Person: Mrs. Jean Sawyer Weaver
Geographic Giving Pattern: Nationwide
Special Interest: Protestant church support, religious associations,
   education, welfare funds

SCHMIDT (MARJORIE MOSHER) FOUNDATION
15795 Rockfield, Suite G
Irvine, CA 92714
(714) 951-1203

Contact Person: Mark F. Scudder, Secretary
Geographic Giving Pattern: Nationwide
Special Interest: Christian religious organizations. Also social,
   health, welfare organizations and education

SMITH (THE MAY AND STANLEY) TRUST
c/o John P. Collins, Sr.
49 Geary Street, Suite 244
San Francisco, CA 94102
(415) 391-0292

Contact Person: John P. Collins, Sr.
Geographic Giving Pattern: San Francisco area. Also in England,
  Scotland, Canada and Australia
Special Interest: Church support and religious welfare funds

STAMPS (JAMES L.) FOUNDATION, INC.
P.O. Box 250
Downey, CA 90241
(213) 861-3112

Contact Person: Milan Green, Secretary
Geographic Giving Pattern: West Coast states and Arizona
Special Interest: Evangelical Protestant churches, seminaries,
  associations and programs

VOSE (CLARA EDITH) FOUNDATION
c/o Rimel and Rimel
1055 N. Main Street, Station 406
Santa Ana, CA 92701
(714) 547-7395

Contact Person: Jack J. Rimel, Secretary
Geographic Giving Pattern: Primarily local
Special Interest: Evangelical church support, youth agencies,
  missions

Connecticut

BISSELL (J. WALTON) FOUNDATION
One Constitution Plaza, 12th floor
Hartford, CT 06103
(203) 521-6528

Contact Person: Wm. C. Fenneman, Secretary
Geographic Giving Pattern: National
Special Interest: Protestant church support. Also higher education,
  hospital, agencies for youth and the aged

WHEELER (WILMOT) FOUNDATION, INC.
P.O. Box 429
Southport, CT 06490
(203) 295-1615

Contact Person: Wilmot F. Wheeler, Jr., President
Geographic Giving Pattern: Primarily local
Special Interest: Education, Protestant church support, hospital and
   community funds

Delaware

CHICHESTER DU PONT FOUNDATION, INC.
1080 Du Pont Building
Wilmington, DE 19801
(302) 658-5244

Contact Person: A. Felix Du Pont, Jr., Treasurer
Geographic Giving Pattern: Primarily local
Special Interest: Church support

KENT (THE ADA HOWE) FOUNDATION
100 West Tenth Street
Wilmington, DE 19801

Contact Person: John E. Connelly, President; 299 Park Avenue,
17th floor, New York, NY 10017
Geographic Giving Pattern: National
Special Interest: Religious organizations carrying on studies and
practical work in comparative religions, church support

KENT - LUCAS FOUNDATION, INC.
101 Springer Building
3411 Silverside Road
Wilmington, DE 19801
(302) 478-4383

Contact Person: Mrs. Elizabeth K. Van Alen, President
Geographic Giving Pattern: Primarily in Philadelphia, PA
   and in Maine and Florida
Special Interest: Protestant church support, hospitals, medical and
   health organizations

LOVETT FOUNDATION, INC., THE
82 Governor Printz Blvd.
Claymont, DE 19703
(302) 798-6604

Contact Person: Michael J. Robinson, III, Vice-President
Geographic Giving Pattern: Delaware and Pennsylvania
Special Interest: Protestant church support, education, cultural and
   civic affairs

WARE FOUNDATION, THE
3908 Kennett Pike, Greenville
Wilmington, DE 19807
(302) 656-1681

Contact Person: The Ware Foundation (above address)
Geographic Giving Pattern: Pennsylvania, North Carolina, Florida
Special Interest: Religious and civic organizations with emphasis on
   higher education, hospitals, health agencies, child welfare and
   Presbyterian church support

District of Columbia

APPLEBY FOUNDATION, THE
c/o Trust Division, National Savings & Trust Bank
15th Street and New York Ave., N.W.
Washington, D.C. 20005
(202) 383-8538

Contact Person: Trust Div. - National Savings & Trust Bank
Geographic Giving Pattern: Washington, D.C., Florida, Georgia
Special Interest: Protestant church support. Also higher education,
   hospitals, cultural programs

MARRIOTT (THE J. WILLARD) FAMILY FOUNDATION
One Marriott Drive, N.W.
Washington, D.C. 20058

Contact Person: Sterling D. Colton
Geographic Giving Pattern: National
Special Interest: Mormon church support

STEUART (GUY T.) FOUNDATION, INC.
4646 Fortieth Street, N.W.
Washington, D.C. 20016
(202) 537-8940

Contact Person: Foundation at above address
Geographic Giving Pattern: Primarily local
Special Interest: Higher education, hospitals, youth agencies and
   church suppport

Florida

AURORA FOUNDATION, THE
P.O. Box 1848
Bradenton, FL 33506
(813) 748-4100

Contact Person: Anthony T. Rossi, Chairman
Geographic Giving Pattern: National
Special Interest: Missions and church support, primarily Protestant

BAKER (THE GEORGE T.) FOUNDATION, INC.
P.O. Box 370606, Buena Vista Station
Miami, FL 33137
Contact Person: Mrs. Helen V. Waller, Secretary-Treasurer
Geographic Giving Pattern: Dade County, Florida; Blowing Rock,
    North Carolina
Special Interest: Education, hospitals, health agencies and medical
    research, youth agencies, Protestant church support

BASTIEN FOUNDATION
6991 West Broward Blvd.
Ft. Lauderdale, FL 33317
(305) 791-0810
Contact Person: Foundation at above address
Geographic Giving Pattern: General   National
Special Interest: Church support - Lutheran and Catholic. Also
    higher education, health agencies, general welfare

BIBLE ALLIANCE
P.O. Box 1894
Bradenton, FL 33506
(813) 748-4100
Contact Person: Anthony T. Rossi, Chairman
Special Interest: Production and distribution of recorded portions of
    the Bible and religious messages on cassette tapes in various
    languages for use in missonary outreach

CRANE (THE RAYMOND E. AND ELLEN F.) FOUNDATION
c/o Coopers & Lybrand
150 E. Palmetto Park Road, Suite 400
Boca Raton, FL 33432
Contact Person: Foundation at above address
Geographic Giving Pattern: National
Special Interest: Higher education and community funds. Also
    cultural programs, health and Protestant church support

DAVIS (THE ARTHUR VINING) FOUNDATIONS
Haskell Building, Suite 520
Oak & Fisk Streets
Jacksonville, FL 32204
(904) 359-0670

Contact Person: Max Morris, Executive Director
Geographic Giving Pattern: National
Special Interest: Private higher education, medicine, religious and
  public television

DUDA FOUNDATION, THE
P.O. Box 257
Oviedo, FL 32765
Contact Person: Andrew Duda, Jr., President
Geographic Giving Pattern: National
Special Interest: Protestant church support and church-related
  organizations

FORD (JEFFERSON LEE) III MEMORIAL FOUNDATION, INC.
Sun Bank of Bal Harbour
Bal Harbour, FL 33154
(305) 865-9911
1101 17th Street, N.W.
Washington, D.C. 20036
Contact Person: Herbert L. Kuras - Florida address
Special Interest: Religious institutions, Christian and Jewish

LAMB (KIRKLAND S. AND RENA B.) FOUNDATION, INC.
1312 Eckles Drive
Tampa, FL 33612
Contact Person: Wendell G. Johnston, President
Geographic Giving Pattern: National
Special Interest: Primarily for Protestant church support, church-
  related programs and theological studies

PENTLAND (ROBERT), JR. CHARITABLE TRUST
c/o Barnett Banks Trust Co.
P.O. Box 40200
Jacksonville, FL 32231
(904) 791-7878
Contact Person: Barnett Banks Trust Co.
Special Interest: Christian church support and youth agencies

Georgia

BRADLEY (U.C. AND SARAH H.) FOUNDATION
P.O. Box 140
Columbia, GA 31902
(404) 322-7348

Contact Person: Wm. B. Turner, Chairman
Geographic Giving Pattern: Primarily local
Special Interest: Higher education, Protestant church support, youth and social agencies

CALLAWAY (FULLER E.) FOUNDATION
209 Broom Street
P.O. Box 790
La Grange, GA 30241
(404) 884-7348

Contact Person: J.T. Gresham, Gen. Manager
Geographic Giving Pattern: Local
Special Interest: Religious and educational institutions

CAMPBELL (J. BULOW) FOUNDATION
1401 Trust Company Tower
25 Park Place N.E.
Atlanta, GA 30303
(404) 658-9066

Contact Person: Morris S. Hale, Jr., Executive Director
Geographic Giving Pattern: Limited to Georgia, Alabama, Florida, North Carolina, South Carolina and Tennessee
Special Interest: Southern Presbyterian Church - U.S.

DAY COMPANIES FOUNDATION, INC.
c/o Charles A. Sanders
2751 Buford Highway
Atlanta, GA 30326
(404) 325-4000

Contact Person: Charles A. Sanders, Treasurer
Geographic Giving Pattern: National
Special Interest: Protestant religious organizations, missionary programs, church support

GHOLSTON (J.K.) TRUST
P.O. Box 992
Athens, GA 30603
(404) 549-8700

Contact Person: Trust Officer - Citizens & Southern National Bank, Athens, GA
Geographic Giving Pattern: Local
Special Interest: Church support - primarily Baptist

ILLGES (A. & M.L.) MEMORIAL FOUNDATION, INC.
1345 Second Avenue
P.O. Box 103
Columbus, GA 31902
Contact Person: A. Illges; 1224 Peacock Ave., Columbus, GA,
   (404) 323-5342
Geographic Giving Pattern: Local, Georgia
Special Interest: Church support

PATTERSON - BARCLAY MEMORIAL FOUNDATION, INC.
1020 Spring Street, N.W.
Atlanta, GA 30309
(404) 876-1022
Contact Person: Mrs. Lee Barclay Patterson Allen
Special Interest: Churches and allied organizations; schools,
   including seminaries and schools of theology, primarily Protestant,
   some Roman Catholic and Greek Orthodox

PATTILLO FOUNDATION, THE
2053 Mountain Industrial Blvd.
Tucker, GA 30084
(404) 938-6366
Contact Person: H.G. Pattillo
Geographic Giving Pattern: Primarily local
Special Interest: Higher education and Protestant church support

PITTS (WILLIAM I.H. AND LULA E.) FOUNDATOIN
P.O. Box 4655
Atlanta, GA 30302
(404) 588-8544
Contact Person: Marvin R. Benson, Secretary
Geographic Giving Pattern: Georgia
Special Interest: Primarily Methodist church related institutions

RAGAN & KING CHARITABLE FOUNDATION
P.O. Box 4148
Atlanta, GA 30302
Contact Person: First National Bank of Atlanta
Geographic Giving Pattern: Primarily Local
Special Interest: Baptist church support, religious organizations,
   theological seminaries, higher education

RAINBOW FUND
P.O. Box 937
Fort Valley, GA 31030
(912) 825-2021

Contact Person: Albert L. Luce, Jr., Treasurer
Geographic Giving Pattern: National
Special Interest: Protestant church support, religious organizations, missionary programs, theological education

SEWELL (WARREN P. AND AVA F.) FOUNDATION
Bremen, GA 30110
(404) 537-2391

Contact Person: Raymond C. Otwell, Trustee
Geographic Giving Pattern: Local
Special Interest: Protestant churches, schools

WILSON (THE FRANCES WOOD) FOUNDATION, INC.
P.O. Box 33188
Decatur, GA 30033
(404) 634-3363

Contact Person: Emory K. Crenshaw, President
Geographic Giving Pattern: Primarily local
Special Interest: Christian Science church. Also Methodist church in Tennessee

Hawaii

ATHERTON FAMILY FOUNDATION
P.O. Box 3170
Honolulu, HI 96802
(808) 525-8536

Contact Person: Jane R., Giddings, Secretary
Geographic Giving Pattern: Hawaii
Special Interest: Protestant church support, scholarships for Protestant ministers' children or for theological education

WILCOX (G.N.) TRUST
c/o Bishop Trust Company, Limited
P.O. Box 2390
Honolulu, HI 96804
(808) 523-2111

Contact Person: Mrs. Lois C. Loomis, Charitable Foundation office
Geographic Giving Pattern: Particularly Island of Kauai
Special Interest: Education and child welfare, Protestant church support

Idaho

MORRISON (HARRY W.) FOUNDATION, INC,
c/o Richard L. Thomas
P.O. Box 7808
Boise, ID 83729
(208) 386-5306

Contact Person: Richard L. Thomas, Secretary
Geographic Giving Pattern: Primarily local
Special Interest: Protestant church support. Also higher education, youth agencies, medical research, cultural programs

Illinois

BAUER (M.R.) FOUNDATION
209 S. La Salle Street, Room 777
Chicago, IL 60604
(312) 372-1947

Contact Person: Kent Lawrence, Treasurer
Geographic Giving Pattern: National
Special Interest: Higher education, Protestant church support

CROWELL (HENRY P.) AND SUSAN C. CROWELL TRUST
Continental Illinois National Bank & Trust Co. of Chicago
30 N. La Salle Street
Chicago, IL 60693
(312) 828-5548

Contact Person: Le Roy E. Johnson, Secretary
Geographic Giving Pattern: National, international
Special Interest: To aid evangelical Christianity

HALES CHARITABLE FUND, INC.
120 West Madison Street, Suite 14-B
Chicago, IL 60602
(312) 641-7016

Contact Person: Wm. M. Hales, President
Geographic Giving Pattern: National
Special Interest: Protestant church organizations and health agencies

HARPER (PHILIP S.) FOUNDATION
930 N. York Road
Hinsdale, IL 60521
(312) 325-3400

Contact Person: Charles C. Lamar, Secretary-Treasurer
Geographic Giving Pattern: National
Special Interest: Protestant church support

LAYMAN TRUST FOR EVANGELISM
c/o Robert H. Langerhans, Trustee
2047 Vermont Street
Quincy, IL 62301
(217) 222-2517

Contact Person: Robert H. Langerhans
Special Interest: Protestant evangelical associations for
   missionary work

MARQUETTE CHARITABLE ORGANIZATION
2141 S. Jefferson Street
Chicago, IL 60616
(312) 226-3232

Contact Person: Betty Basile, Secretary-Treasurer
Geographic Giving Pattern: National
Special Interest: Christian religious organizations, churches,
   education

RHOADES (OTTO L. AND HAZEL T.) FUND
c/o Leo J. Carlin
800 Sears Tower
Chicago, IL 60606
(312) 876-8000

Contact Person: Leo J. Carlin
Geographic Giving Pattern: Chicago
Special Interest: Religious support - Presbyterian church, Christian
   communications organizations

TYNDAL HOUSE FOUNDATION
336 Gundersen Drive, Box 80
Wheaton, IL 60187
(312) 293-0179

Contact Person: Mary Kleine Yehling, Executive Director
Geographic Giving Pattern: National
Special Interest: Missions, evangelical organizations, Christian
   literature projects and Bible translation

WERNER (CLARA AND SPENCER) FOUNDATION, INC.
616 S. Jefferson Street
Paris, IL 61944

Contact Person: Clara B. Werner, Chairman
Geographic Giving Pattern: National
Special Interest: Lutheran churches, and programs including
   theological education

Indiana

BALL BROTHERS FOUNDATION
520 Merchants Bank Building
Muncie, IN 47305

Contact Person: Douglas A. Bakken, Executive Director
Geographic Giving Pattern: Indiana
Special Interest: Educational, cultural, religious organizations

SMOCK (FRANK L. AND LAURA L.) FOUNDATION
c/o Lincoln National Bank & Trust Co.
116 E. Berry Street
Fort Wayne, IN 46802
(219) 423-6496

Contact Person: Lincoln National Bank & Trust Co.
Geographic Giving Pattern: Indiana
Special Interest: Presbyterian churches, a college, and ailing or
  needy elderly people

THRUSH (H.A.) FOUNDATION, INC.
P.O. Box 185
Peru, IN 46970
(317) 473-6765

Contact Person: Robert Thompson, Secretary
Geographic Giving Pattern: Primarily local
Special Interest: Protestant church support. Also higher education,
  health agencies, cultural programs

Iowa

E & M CHARITIES
c/o C. Maxwell Stanley
Stanley Building
Muscatine, IA 52761

Contact Person: C. Maxwell Stanley, President
Geographic Giving Pattern: National
Special Interest: Higher education, a Catholic mission, Protestant
  churches particularly Methodist

STRAUB FOUNDATION
1922 Ingersoll Avenue
Des Moines, IA 50309

Contact Person: Edward Lockner, President
Geographic Giving Pattern: Primarily Local
Special Interest: Higher education, Christian religious organizations

Kansas

NELSON (THE LUDVIG AND SELMA) RELIGIOUS, EDUCATIONAL AND CHARITABLE TRUST
Kansas and Maple (Pioneer Building)
McPherson, KS 67460
(316) 241-0554

Contact Person: Robert W. Wise, Trustee
Geographic Giving Pattern: Kansas
Special Interest: Non-tax supported institutions. Emphasis on higher education, hospitals, Protestant churches

WIEDEMANN (K.T.) FOUNDATION, INC.
8615 Shannon Way
Wichita, KS 67206
(316) 685-5252

Contact Person: Gladys H.G. Wiedemann, President and Trustee
Geographic Giving Pattern: Primarily local
Special Interest: Church support

Kentucky

COOKE (V.V.) FOUNDATION CORPORATION
3901 Atkinson Drive, Suite 409
Louisville, KY 40218
(502) 459-3968

Contact Person: Charles H. Wells, Executive Secretary
Geographic Giving Pattern: Primarily local
Special Interest: Baptist church support and higher education

HOUCHENS FOUNDATION, INC.
900 Church Street
Bowling Green, KY 42101
(502) 843-3252

Contact Person: E.G. Houchens, Chairman
Geographic Giving Pattern: Primarily local
Special Interest: Church support

LA VIERS (HARRY AND MAXIE) FOUNDATION, INC.
P.O. Box 332
Irvine, KY 40336
(606) 723-5111

Contact Person: Barbara P. La Viers, Secretary-Treasurer
Geographic Giving Pattern: Primarily local
Special Interest: Protestant church support and higher education

Louisiana

FRAZIER FOUNDATION, INC.
P.O. Box 1175
Minden, LA 71055
(318) 377-0182

Contact Person: James Walter Frazier, Jr., President
Geographic Giving Pattern: National
Special Interest: Church of Christ churches, missions, religious
 organizations, educational institutions

WHELESS FOUNDATION, THE
c/o Commercial National Bank in Shreveport
P.O. Box 21119
Shreveport, LA 71152
(318) 226-4631

Contact Person: Nicholas H. Wheless, Jr., Chairman
Geographic Giving Pattern: Primarily local
Special Interest: Church support

Maryland

CLARK-WINCHCOLE FOUNDATION
7315 Wisconsin Avenue, Suite 410E
Bethesda, MD 20814
(301) 654-3607

Contact Person: Charles Emory Phillips, President
Geographic Giving Pattern: Primarily Washington, D.C. area
Special Interest: Higher education - all denominations, health and
 youth agencies, medical research and hospitals, Protestant church
 support

M.E. FOUNDATION, THE
Rutherford Plaza
7133 Rutherford Road
Baltimore, MD 21207

Contact Person: Mrs. Margaret Brown Trimble, President and
 Secretary
Geographic Giving Pattern: National, international
Special Interest: Protestant evangelistic missionary work and
 Bible studies

Michigan

CHAMBERLIN (GERALD W.) FOUNDATION, INC.
18301 E. Eight Mile Road, Suite 212
E. Detroit, MI 48021
(313) 777-3820

Contact Person: Catherine M. Hoyer, Secretary
Geographic Giving Pattern: Primarily local
Special Interest: Protestant church support, youth agencies, higher and secondary education

COOK (PETER C. AND EMAJEAN) CHARITABLE TRUST
c/o Peter C. Cook
2660 28th Street, S.E.
Grand Rapids, MI 49506
(616) 949-7788

Contact Person: Peter C. Cook, Trustee
Geographic Giving Pattern: Primarily local
Special Interest: Protestant religious organizations, theological seminary, higher education

DE VOS (THE RICHARD AND HELEN) FOUNDATION
7154 Windy Hill Road, S.E.
Grand Rapids, MI 49506

Contact Person: Richard M. De Vos, President
Geographic Giving Pattern: National
Special Interest: Evangelical organizations and churches

HERRICK FOUNDATION
2500 Detroit Bank and Trust Building
Detroit, MI 48226
(313) 963-6420

Contact Person: Emmett E. Eagan, Vice-President and Secretary
Geographic Giving Pattern: Primarily local, some national
Special Interest: Protestant church support, health and welfare agencies, higher and secondary education

LA-Z-BOY CHAIR FOUNDATION
1284 N. Telegraph Road
P.O. Box 713
Monroe, MI 48161
(313) 242-1444

Contact Person: Herman Gertz, Administrator
Geographic Giving Pattern: National (in areas of company operations)
Special Interest: Church support

PAGEL (WILLIAM M. AND MARY E.) TRUST
c/o National Bank of Detroit
611 Woodward Avenue
Detroit, MI 48232
(313) 225-2764

Contact Person: Edwin R. Stroh, III, Manager, National Bank
of Detroit
Geographic Giving Pattern: Local, Detroit
Special Interest: Protestant church support

Mississippi

COMMUNITY FOUNDATION, INC, THE
P.O. Box 924
Jackson, MS 39205

Contact Person: W.K. Paine, President-Treasurer
Geographic Giving Pattern: Primarily local
Special Interest: Protestant religious organizations, higher education
and social agencies

Missouri

PILLSBURY FOUNDATION, THE
Six Oakleigh Lane
St. Louis, MO 63124

Contact Person: Joyce S. Pillsbury, President
Geographic Giving Pattern: Local, some national
Special Interest: Higher education, Baptist church support and
religious organizations

WOLFF (THE JOHN M.) FOUNDATION
c/o Tower Grove Bank and Trust Company
3134 South Grand Boulevard
St. Louis, MO 63118

Contact Person: Edith D. Wolff, Trustee
Geographic Giving Pattern: Primarily Local
Special Interest: Church support, higher education, health agencies

New Hampshire

STANDEX FOUNDATION OF NEW YORK, INC.
6 Manor Parkway
Salem, NH 03079
(603) 893-9701

Contact Person: Thomas L. King, President-Treasurer
Geographic Giving Pattern: National
Special Interest: Church support and church-related organizations,
  missions

New Jersey

KIRBY (F.M.) FOUNDATION, INC
17 De Hart Street
Morristown, NJ 07960
(201) 538-4800

Contact Person: F.M. Kirby II, President
Geographic Giving Pattern: Primarily New Jersey, New York,
  Pennsylvania
Special Interest: Education, church support, church-related
  organizations

WILLITS FOUNDATION, THE
731 Central Avenue
Murray Hill, NJ 07974
(201) 277-8259

Contact Person: Harris L. Willits, President
Geographic Giving Pattern: New Jersey, Georgia, Maine,
  New Mexico, New York and Massachusetts
Special Interest: Protestant church support, theological seminaries,
  higher education especially for the ministry

New York

BAIRD FOUNDATION, THE
1880 Elmwood Avenue
Buffalo, NY 14207
(716) 876-8100

Contact Person: William C. Baird, Manager
Geographic Giving Pattern: Primarily Erie County, New York
Special Interest: Episcopal church support

CHATLOS FOUNDATION, INC., THE
2 Pennsylvania Plaza, Room 1648
New York, NY 10121
(212) 736-4343

Contact Person: William J. Chatlos, President
Geographic Giving Pattern: National
Special Interest: Higher education including religious education and
  religious associations

DEWAR (JAMES AND JESSIE SMITH) FOUNDATION, INC.
177 Main Street
Oneonta, NY 13820
Contact Person: Ruston R. Henderson, President and Treasurer
Geographic Giving Pattern: Primarily local
Special Interest: Religious, charitable, cultural, educational purposes.

KLEE (THE CONRAD AND VIRGINIA) FOUNDATION, INC.
c/o Clayton M. Axtell, Jr.
First City Division of Lincoln First Bank
Binghamton, NY 13902
(607) 772-2261
Contact Person: Clayton M. Axtell, Jr., President
Geographic Giving Pattern: Local, Broom County, Guilford in
  Chenango County
Special Interest: Community funds, Protestant church support,
  higher education

KNOX GELATINE FOUNDATION
P.O. Box 387
Johnstown, NY 12095
Contact Person: John B. Knox, Chairman
Geographic Giving Pattern: National
Special Interest: Educational, civic, medical, Protestant
  church support

MOSTYN FOUNDATION, INC.
c/o J.F. Lambert
645 Madison Avenue, Suite 1800
New York, NY 10022
(212) 832-3919
Contact Person: Mrs. Whitney B. Atwood, President
Geographic Giving Pattern: National
Special Interest: Church support, evangelical organizations

PALMER (FRANCIS ASBURY) FUND
c/o William A. Chisolm
47 E. 88th Street
New York, NY 10028
(212) 348-3100
Contact Person: William A. Chisolm, Secretary
Geographic Giving Pattern: National, international
Special Interest: Home missions and educational institutions,
  Christian ministers and workers, establishment of Bible teaching
  in colleges and schools, theological education

SPRAGUE (THE SETH) EDUCATIONAL AND CHARITABLE FOUNDATION
c/o U.S. Trust Co. of New York
45 Wall Street
New York, NY 10005
(212) 425-4500

Contact Person: Mrs. Maureen Augusciak, Vice-President
Geographic Giving Pattern: New York and Massachusetts
Special Interest: Church support, theological seminaries, education, medical research, aid to the handicapped

WALKER (THE GEORGE HERBERT) FOUNDATION
101 Park Avenue
New York, NY 10178
(212) 697-4100

Contact Person: Winslow M. Lovejoy
Geographic Giving Pattern: Eastern United States
Special Interest: Higher and secondary education, Protestant church support

WENDT (THE MARGARET L.) FOUNDATION
1325 Liberty Bank Building
Buffalo, NY 14203
(716) 855-2146

Contact Person: Robert J. Kresse, Secretary
Geographic Giving Pattern: Primarily local
Special Interest: Lutheran church support. Also religious organizations

North Carolina

ANDERSON (ROBERT C. AND SADIE G.) FOUNDATION
c/o North Carolina National Bank
Charlotte, NC 28255
(704) 374-5721

Contact Person: John F. Renger, Jr.
Geographic Giving Pattern: North Carolina
Special Interest: Presbyterian causes or institutions

BELK FOUNDATION, THE
308 E. Fifth Street
P.O. Box 2727
Charlotte, NC 28234

Contact Person: Thomas M. Belk, Chairman
Geographic Giving Pattern: North Carolina and South Carolina
Special Interest: Protestant church support, higher education

CANNON FOUNDATION, INC., THE
P.O. Box 467
Concord, NC 28025
Contact Person: T.C. Haywood, Secretary-Treasurer
Geographic Giving Pattern: Primarily local
Special Interest: Protestant church support, schools, hospitals

DOVER FOUNDATION, INC., THE
P.O. Box 208
Shelby, NC 28150
Contact Person: Charles I. Dover, President
Geographic Giving Pattern: Primarily local
Special Interest: Protestant church support. Also higher and
  secondary education

MORGAN TRUST FOR CHARITY, RELIGION AND
  EDUCATION
Laurel Hill, NC 28351
(919) 462-2016
Contact Person: James L. Morgan, Chairman
Geographic Giving Pattern: Primarily local
Special Interest: Higher education, a theological seminary, Protestant
  church support

RICHARDSON (THE MARY LYNN) FUND
P.O. Box 20124
Greensboro, NC 27420
(919) 274-5471
Contact Person: James F. Connolly, Manager
Geographic Giving Pattern: International
Special Interest: Foreign missions for religious, charitable or
  educational application

STOWE (ROBERT LEE) JR. FOUNDATION, INC.
P.O. Box 351
Mill Office Building
Belmont, NC 28012
Contact Person: Robert Lee Stowe, Jr., President
Geographic Giving Pattern: Primarily local
Special Interest: Church support, child welfare, education

Ohio

AUSTIN MEMORIAL FOUNDATION, THE
3650 Mayfield Road
Cleveland Heights, OH 44118

Contact Person: Donald G. Austin, Jr., President
Geographic Giving Pattern: Primarily local
Special Interest: Higher and secondary education, hospitals,
  Protestant church support

CROSSET CHARITABLE TRUST, THE
205 Central Avenue
Cincinnati, OH 45202
(513) 421-5511

Contact Person: Richard B. Crosset, Trustee
Geographic Giving Pattern: Primarily local
Special Interest: Religious, charitable, educational purposes

MLM CHARITABLE FOUNDATION
410 United Savings Building
Toledo, OH 43604
(419) 255-0500

Contact Person: Mary L. McKenny, President
Geographic Giving Pattern: National
Special Interest: Higher education, Protestant churches and
  ministries

MOORES (THE HARRY C.) FOUNDATION
c/o F.E. Caldwell
866 Clubview Boulevard
Worthington, OH 43085
(614) 221-6651

Contact Person: William H. Leighner, Secretary; 100 E. Broad St.,
  Columbus, OH 43215
Geographic Giving Pattern: Primarily Columbus, Ohio, area
Special Interest: Rehabilitation of the handicapped, Protestant
  church support, hospitals, welfare organizations and
  cultural programs

TELL (PAUL P.) FOUNDATION
2762 Mayfair Road
Akron, OH 44312
(216) 614-7531

Contact Person: David J. Schipper, President
Geographic Giving Pattern: National
Special Interest: Furtherance of evangelical Christianity

Oklahoma

BROADHURST FOUNDATION
5350 E. 46th Street, Suite 116
P.O. Box 35858
Tulsa, OK 74135
(918) 663-9251

Contact Person: Ernestine Broadhurst Howard, Trustee
Geographic Giving Pattern: Mid-west
Special Interest: Scholarship funds for students training for the
  Christian ministry, support for educational and religious
  institutions

PUTERBAUGH FOUNDATION
P.O. Box 729
McAlester, OK 74501
(918) 426-1591

Contact Person: Don C. Phelps, Managing Trustee
Geographic Giving Pattern: Primarily local
Special Interest: Unitarian religious associations

TULSA ROYALTIES COMPANY
3229-A S. Harvard Avenue
Tulsa, OK 74135
(918) 747-5638

Contact Person: William S. Bailey, Jr., President
Geographic Giving Pattern: Primarily local
Special Interest: Higher education, hospitals, social agencies,
  Protestant church support

Pennsylvania

ADAMS FOUNDATION, INC.
202 W. Fourth Street
Bethlehem, PA 18016
(215) 867-5000; Ext. 241

Contact Person: Nancy A. Taylor, President
Geographic Giving Pattern: National
Special Interest: Higher and secondary education, hospitals,
  Protestant church support

ASPLUNDH FOUNDATION
Blair Mill Road
Willow Grove, PA 19090

Contact Person: Lester Asplundh, President
Geographic Giving Pattern: Primarily local
Special Interest: Protestant church support

CRAIG (EARLE M.) AND MARGARET PETERS CRAIG TRUST
c/o Mellon Bank
Mellon Square
Pittsburgh, PA 15230
(412) 234-5784

Contact Person: Barbara K. Robinson, Asst. Vice-President
Geographic Giving Pattern: National
Special Interest: Higher education, Protestant churches and
  religious organizations

CRAWFORD (E.R.) ESTATE TRUST FUND A
P.O. Box 487
McKeesport, PA 15134

Contact Person: Francis E. Neish, Trustee
Geographic Giving Pattern: Primarily McKeesport and Duquesne,
  Pennsylvania
Special Interest: Protestant church support

HILLMAN (THE HENRY L.) FOUNDATION
2000 Grant Building
Pittsburgh, PA 15219
(412) 566-1480

Contact Person: Ronald W. Wertz, Executive Director
Geographic Giving Pattern: Primarily Pittsburgh
Special Interest: Episcopal church support

HUSTON FOUNDATION, THE
c/o The Glenmede Trust Co.
229 S. 18th Street
Philadelphia, PA 19103
(215) 875-3200

Contact Person: John Van Gorder
Geographic Giving Pattern: National
Special Interest: Evangelical organizations

PETERS (CHARLES F.) FOUNDATION
c/o Equibank
2 Oliver Plaza
Pittsburgh, PA 15222
(412) 288-5638

Contact Person: J. Charles Peterson, Administrator
Geographic Giving Pattern: McKeesport area
Special Interest: Protestant church support

PEW (J. HOWARD) FREEDOM TRUST
c/o The Glenmede Trust Co.
229 S. 18th Street
Philadelphia, PA 19103
(215) 875-3200
Contact Person: Fred H. Billups, Jr., Vice-President
Geographic Giving Pattern: National
Special Interest: Christian religious organizations and
  theological seminaries

PITCAIRN-CRABBE FOUNDATION
301 Fifth Avenue, Suite 1417
Pittsburgh, PA 15222
(412) 391-5122
Contact Person: Alfred W. Wishart, Executive Secretary
Geographic Giving Pattern: Local, western Pennsylvania,
  especially Pittsburgh
Special Interest: Christian education, Protestant religious and
  church work

SCHAUTZ (THE WALTER L.) FOUNDATION
150 E. Grove Street
Dunmore, PA 18512
(717) 344-1174
Contact Person: Madalene Schautz, President
Geographic Giving Pattern: Local
Special Interest: Theological seminaries, church support

STACKPOLE-HALL FOUNDATION
19 N. St. Marys Street
St. Marys, PA 15857
(814) 781-1167
Contact Person: William C. Conrad, Executive Secretary
Geographic Giving Pattern: Primarily Pennsylvania, some in
  Massachusetts, North Carolina, Connecticut, New York,
  Washington, D.C.
Special Interest: Religion, especially Episcopal,education, charity

Rhode Island

HAFFENREFFER FAMILY FUND
c/o Fleet National Bank
100 Westminster Street
Providence, RI 02903
(401) 278-6697

Contact Person: Fleet National Bank, Trustee
Geographic Giving Pattern: Rhode Island and southeastern
    New England
Special Interest: Protestant church support

South Carolina

BELK-SIMPSON FOUNDATION
P.O. Box 1449
Greenville, SC 29602

Contact Person: Mrs. Willou Bichel, Director: P.O. Box 528,
    Greenville, SC 29602
Geographic Giving Pattern: Local
Special Interest: Protestant church support and higher
    education

SIMPSON FOUNDATION, THE
c/o C & S National Bank of South Carolina
P.O. Box 1449
Greenville, SC 29602
(801) 271-4112

Contact Person: Mrs. Willou Bichel, Director
Geographic Giving Pattern: Primarily North and South Carolina
Special Interest: Protestant church support and religious
    organizations

STEVENS (JOHN T.) FOUNDATION
P.O. Box 158
Kershaw, SC 29067
(803) 475-3655

Contact Person: John S. Davidson, President
Geographic Giving Pattern: Primarily local
Special Interest: Protestant church support

Tennessee

BROWN (THE DORA MACLELLAN) CHARITABLE TRUST
1023 James Building
Chatanooga, TN 37402
(615) 266-5257

Contact Person: W. Henry Trotter, President
Geographic Giving Pattern: Primarily local, and the south east
Special Interest: Education, Protestant religious associations
and hospitals

CHURCH OF CHRIST FOUNDATION, INC.
224 Second Avenue N.
P.O. Box 1301
Nashville, TN 37202
(615) 244-0600

Contact Person: Paul A. Hargis, President
Geographic Giving Pattern: National
Special Interest: Church of Christ related organizations including
churches, schools and colleges

HYDE (J.R.) FOUNDATION, INC.
1991 Corporate Avenue
Memphis, TN 38132

Contact Person: Ms. Margaret Hyde, President
Geographic Giving Pattern: Mid-South area of United States
Special Interest: Missions, church support, education

MACLELLAN FOUNDATION, INC., THE
Provident Building
Chattanooga, TN 37402
(615) 755-1251

Contact Person: Hugh O. Maclellan, Jr., President
Geographic Giving Pattern: Primarily local
Special Interest: Evangelical church support, theological seminaries

Texas

ADAMS (THE MOODY) FOUNDATION
5002 Happy Hollow
Houston, TX 77018
Contact Person: Mrs. Marcene H. Adams, Vice-President
Geographic Giving Pattern: Texas and Mississippi
Special Interest: Education and Protestant church support

AKIN FOUNDATION, THE
P.O. Box 19429
Houston, TX 77024
(713) 932-6210

Contact Person: James D. Yates, Secretary
Geographic Giving Pattern: Texas
Special Interest: Aid to various Churches of Christ

ALLBRITTON (THE JOE L. AND BARBARA B.) FOUNDATION
5615 Kirby Drive, Suite 310
Houston, TX 77005
(713) 522-4921

Contact Person: Virginia L. White, Secretary-Treasurer
Geographic Giving Pattern: Texas, New York, Washington, D.C.
Special Interest: Christian religious organizations and education

BEASLEY (THEODORE AND BEULAH) FOUNDATION, INC.
Two Turtle Creek Village, Suite 422
Dallas, TX 75219
(214) 522-8790

Contact Person: Theodore P. Beasley, President
Geographic Giving Pattern: Primarily local
Special Interest: Higher education, including theological seminaries
   and Protestant church support

BELL TRUST
10726 Plano Road
Dallas, TX 75238
(214) 349-0060

Contact Person: H.L. Packer, Trustee
Geographic Giving Pattern: National, international
Special Interest: Churches of Christ

BIVINS (MARY E.) FOUNDATION
414 Polk Street
P.O. Box 708
Amarillo, TX 79105

Contact Person: Terry Odom, President and Executive Director
Geographic Giving Pattern: Primarily local
Special Interest: Christian colleges, social agencies, health care

BROWN (M.K.) FOUNDATION, INC.
c/o Bill Waters
P.O. Box 662
Pampa, TX 79065
(806) 669-6851

Contact Person: Bill W. Waters, Chairman
Geographic Giving Pattern: Primarily local
Special Interest: Protestant church support

FAIR (THE R.W.) FOUNDATION
P.O. Box 689
Tyler, TX 75710
(214) 592-3811

Contact Person: Wilton H. Fair, President
Geographic Giving Pattern: Primarily local
Special Interest: Protestant church support and church-related
  programs

FIKES (LELAND) FOUNDATION, INC.
3200 Republic National Bank Tower
Dallas, TX 75201
(214) 741-4737

Contact Person: Lee Fikes, President
Geographic Giving Pattern: Primarily local
Special Interest: Protestant church support, medical and social
  research, education

FLEMING FOUNDATION, THE
1007 First National Bank Building
Fort Worth, TX 76102
(817) 335-3741

Contact Person: F. Howard Walsh, Vice-President
Geographic Giving Pattern: Primarily local
Special Interest: Protestant church support and church-related
  activities including radio and TV programs, music,
  higher education

HEATH (ED AND MARY) FOUNDATION
P.O. Box 338
Tyler, TX 75710
(214) 597-7435

Contact Person: W.R. Smith, Chairman
Geographic Giving Pattern: Primarily local
Special Interest: Church support

LE TOURNEAU FOUNDATION, THE
P.O. Box 736
Rockwall, TX 75087
(214) 722-8325

Contact Person: R.S. Le Tourneau, President
Special Interest: Evangelical Christian activities in foreign missions, evangelism, and education

MCCRELESS (SOLLIE AND LILLA) FOUNDATION FOR CHRISTIAN EVANGELISM, CHRISTIAN MISSIONS AND CHRISTIAN EDUCATION
P.O. Box 2341
San Antonio, TX 78298
Contact Person: Marjorie Roese, Secretary-Treasurer
Geographic Giving Pattern: National, some emphasis on San Antonio
Special Interest: Protestant churches, theological education and evangelical organizations

MCMILLAN (BRUCE) JR.,FOUNDATION
P.O. Box 297
Overton, TX 75684
(214) 834-3530
Contact Person: Ralph Ward, Managing Trustee
Geographic Giving Pattern: Local, east Texas
Special Interest: Church support

OLDHAM LITTLE CHURCH FOUNDATION
2200 S. Post Oak Blvd., Suite 405
Houston, TX 77056
(713) 621-4190
Contact Person: Harry A. Kinney, Executive Vice-President
Geographic Giving Pattern: National, international
Special Interest: To aid small Protestant churches and religious educational institutions

TRULL FOUNDATION, THE
404 Fourth Street
P.O. Box 940
Palacios, TX 77465
(512) 972-5241
Contact Person: Coleen Claybourn, Trustee
Geographic Giving Pattern: National
Special Interest: Religious, educational, medical, evangelical purposes

Virginia

ENGLISH (W.C.) FOUNDATION
Altavista, VA 24517
(804) 324-7241

Contact Person: W.C. English, Manager
Geographic Giving Pattern: Primarily local
Special Interest: Religious, educational, civic purposes

OLSSON (ELIS) MEMORIAL FOUNDATION
c/o Carle E. Davis
1400 Ross Building
Richmond, VA 23219

Contact Person: Sture G. Olsson, Manager
Geographic Giving Pattern: Primarily local
Special Interest: Protestant church support, higher and secondary
  education

TITMUS FOUNDATION, INC., THE
Route 1, Box 358
Sutherland, VA 23885

Contact Person: Edward B. Titmus, President
Geographic Giving Pattern: Primarily local
Special Interest: Baptist church support and religious organizations

TREAKLE (THE J. EDWIN) FOUNDATION, INC.
Box 1157
Gloucester, VA 23061

Contact Person: John W. Cooke, Manager
Geographic Giving Pattern: Primarily local
Special Interest: Protestant church support

Washington

STEWARDSHIP FOUNDATION, THE
P.O. Box 1278
Tacoma, WA 98401
(206) 272-8336

Contact Person: C. David Weyerhaeuser,Trustee
Geographic Giving Pattern: No stated restrictions
Special Interest: Protestant theological education and Christian
  evangelical activities

WEYERHAEUSER (C. DAVIS) TRUST
P.O. Box 1278
Tacoma, WA 98401
(206) 272-8336

Contact Person: C. Davis Weyerhaeuser, Trustee
Geographic Giving Pattern: National, international
Special Interest: Evangelical Protestant organizations

Wisconsin

KURTH RELIGIOUS TRUST
2100 S. 43rd Street
Milwaukee, WI 53219
(414) 384-3030

Contact Person: Katherine Kurth, Manager
Geographic Giving Pattern: Primarily local
Special Interest: Lutheran church support and religious associations.
  Also higher education

RODDIS (HAMILTON) FOUNDATION, INC.
c/o Augusta D. Roddis
1108 E. Fourth Street
Marshfield, WI 54449

Contact Person: Augusta D. Roddis, Secretary-Treasurer
Geographic Giving Pattern: National
Special Interest: Episcopal church support, church-related
  institutions, medical research

SIEBERT LUTHERAN FOUNDATION, INC.
2600 North Mayfair Road, Suite 390
Wauwatosa, WI 53226
(414) 257-2656

Contact Person: Jack S. Harris, President
Geographic Giving Pattern: Primarily Wisconsin, some national
Special Interest: Lutheran churches, hospitals, colleges and schools,
  youth agencies and other religious welfare agencies

YOUNG (IRVIN L.) FOUNDATION, INC.
Snow Valley Ranch
Palmyra, WI 53156
(414) 495-2568

Contact Person: Mrs. Fern D. Young, President
Geographic Giving Pattern: International
Special Interest: Protestant medical missionary programs in Africa

Catholic Foundations

Arkansas

WRAPE FAMILY CHARITABLE TRUST, THE
P.O. Box 412
Little Rock, AR 72203
(501) 375-2361
Contact Person: A.J. Wrape, Jr., Trustee
Special Interest: Roman Catholic educational and religious
  organizations

California

BURNS (FRITZ B.) FOUNDATION
4001 West Alameda Avenue, Suite 203
Burbank, CA 91505
(213) 938-7221
Contact Person: Mr. W.K. Skinner, Secretary-Treasurer
Geographic Giving Pattern: Primarily local
Special Interest: Roman Catholic religious associations, hospitals,
  church support

CALLISON FOUNDATION, THE
c/o Feeney, Sparks and Rudy
Hearst Building, Suite 1100
San Francisco, CA 94103
(415) 362-2981
Contact Person: Mrs. Dorothy Sola, Secretary
Geographic Giving Pattern: Primarily local
Special Interest: Roman Catholic religious organizations,
  higher education

DOHENY (CARRIE ESTELLE) FOUNDATION
714 W. Olympic Blvd., Room 510
Los Angeles, CA 90015
(213) 748-5111
Contact Person: Very Rev. W.G. Ward, C.M., Chairman
Geographic Giving Pattern: Local, primarily southern California
Special Interest: Roman Catholic churches and church-related
  organizations, hospitals, ophthalmological research, child welfare,
  education, community funds

DRUM FOUNDATION, THE
c/o Wells Fargo Bank
420 Montgomery #954
San Francisco, CA 94163
(415) 396-3105

Contact Person: Richard K. Miller, President
Geographic Giving Pattern: Usually limited to the Archdiocese of San Francisco
Special Interest: Roman Catholic church-related educational and charitable organizations

FOLEYS (EDWARD T.) FOUNDATION
202 S. Lake Avenue, Suite 330
Pasadena, CA 91001
(213) 684-2401

Contact Person: Jean Foley, Trustee
Geographic Giving Pattern: Primarily California
Special Interest: Missions, church support

GALLO (THE JULIO R.) FOUNDATION
P.O. Box 1130
Modesto, CA 95353
(209) 521-3091

Contact Person: Jon B. Shastid, Treasurer
Geographic Giving Pattern: Primarily local
Special Interest: Roman Catholic church support, religious associations, education

GELLERT (THE CARL) FOUNDATION
2222 Nineteenth Avenue
San Francisco, CA 94116
(415) 566-4420

Contact Person: Peter J. Brusati, Secretary
Geographic Giving Pattern: Primarily local
Special Interest: The aged and hospitals. Also Roman Catholic church support, higher and secondary education

GLEASON (JAMES) FOUNDATION
Hearst Building, Suite 1200
Third and Market Streets
San Francisco, CA 94103
(415) 421-6995

Contact Person: Walter M. Gleason, President
Geographic Giving Pattern: Primarily local
Special Interest: Roman Catholic welfare funds and church support

GLEASON (KATHERINE) FOUNDATION
c/o Walter Gleason
Hearst Building, Suite 1200
Third and Market Streets
San Francisco, CA 94103
(415) 421-6995

Contact Person: Walter M. Gleason, President
Geographic Giving Pattern: World wide
Special Interest: Roman Catholic religious, welfare, educational and
  missionary endeavors

HALE (CRESCENT PORTER) FOUNDATION
251 Kearney Street, Room 408
San Francisco, CA 94108

Contact Person: Melvin M. Swig, President
Special Interest: Higher education, hospitals and Roman Catholic
  religious organizations

HARNEY FOUNDATION, THE
923 Folsom Street
San Francisco, CA 94107
(415) 495-5352

Contact Person: Mrs. P.E. Harney, President
Geographic Giving Pattern: Primarily local
Special Interest: Roman Catholic religious, charitable and
  educational organizations. Also grants for medical and research
  organizations

HAYDEN (WILLIAM R.) FOUNDATION
110 West Las Tunis Drive, Suite A
San Gabriel, CA 91776
(213) 285-9891

Contact Person: William R. Hayden, President
Geographic Giving Pattern: Primarily local, some national
Special Interest: Religious, educational, medical organizations

LEAVEY (THOMAS AND DOROTHY) FOUNDATION
4680 Wilshire Boulevard
Los Angeles, CA 90036
(213) 936-5875

Contact Person: Dorothy Leavey, Vice-President
Geographic Giving Pattern: Primarily local
Special Interest: Roman Catholic church groups, hospitals, medical
  research, higher and secondary education

LEONARDT FOUNDATION
1801 Avenue of the Stars, Suite 500
Los Angeles, CA 90067
(213) 556-3932

Contact Person: Felix S. McGinnis, President
Geographic Giving Pattern: Primarily local
Special Interest: Roman Catholic church support

MULLER (FRANK), SR. FOUNDATION
c/o Norby, Sutherland & Muller
7080 Hollywood Blvd., #305
Hollywood, CA 90028
(213) 463-8176

Contact Person: Frank Muller
Geographic Giving Pattern: Primarily local
Special Interest: Roman Catholic church support, higher and
    secondary education, social agencies, hospitals, cultural programs

MURPHY (DAN) FOUNDATION
P.O. Box 76026
Los Angeles, CA 90076

Contact Person: Daniel J. Donohue
Geographic Giving Pattern: National
Special Interest: Roman Catholic educational, religious, charitable
    organizations

SHEA FOUNDATION, THE
655 Brea Canyon Road
Walnut, CA 91789
(714) 594-9500

Contact Person: John F. Shea, President
Geographic Giving Pattern: California
Special Interest: Roman Catholic church and religious associations.
    Also educationl, civic, cultural endeavors and help for the Blind

TRUST FUNDS, INC.
100 Broadway, Third Floor
San Francisco, CA 94111
(415) 434-3323

Contact Person: Albert J. Steiss
Geographic Giving Pattern: National, international
Special Interest: Roman Catholic institutions and projects which
    promote the religious, educational, and social welfare of all people

VON DER AHE FOUNDATION
4605 Lankershim Blvd., Suite 707
N. Hollywood, CA 91602
(213) 877-2454

Contact Person: Wilfred L. Von der Ahe
Geographic Giving Pattern: Primarily local, some national
Special Interest: Roman Catholic religious institutions and health and welfare services

WELK (LAWRENCE) FOUNDATION
1299 Ocean Avenue, Suite 800
Santa Monica, CA 90401
(213) 451-5727

Contact Person: Theodore Lennon, Secretary-Treasurer
Geographic Giving Pattern: Primarily local
Special Interest: Education, cancer research, hospitals, Roman Catholic institutions, community funds

Colorado

MULLEN (THE JOHN K. AND CATHERINE S.) BENEVOLENT CORPORATION
1345 First National Bank Building
Denver, CO 80202
(303) 893-3151

Contact Person: Leon A. Lascor, Secretary
Geographic Giving Pattern: Primarily local
Special Interest: Public charities and educational institutions with emphasis on church affiliated organizations

WECKBAUGH (ELEANOR MULLEN) FOUNDATION
1345 First National Bank Building
Denver, CO 80202
(303) 893-3151

Contact Person: Leon A. Lascor, President
Geographic Giving Pattern: Primarily local
Special Interest: Roman Catholic church support and welfare funds

Connecticut

CASEY (THE ANNIE E.) FOUNDATION
51 Weaver Street
Greenwich Office Park 5
Greenwich, CT 06830
(203) 622-6095

Contact Person: Annie E. Casey Foundation
Geographic Giving Pattern: Connecticut and Seattle, Washington
Special Interest: Child welfare - specifically the care of foster
children in Connecticut. Also Roman Catholic church support
  in Seattle, Washington

DELL, (THE HAZEL) FOUNDATION
c/o Carroll, Lane & Reed
P.O. Box 771
Norwalk, CT 06852
(203) 853-6565

Contact Person: June M. Powers, President
Geographic Giving Pattern: National
Special Interest: Roman Catholic church support, hospitals,
  education, aid to the handicapped.

HUISKING FOUNDATION, INC., THE
Greenwich Office Park 1
Greenwich, CT 06836
(203) 622-1500

Contact Person: William W. Huisking, Vice-President
Geographic Giving Pattern: General
Special Interest: Education, Roman Catholic church and welfare
  funds, hospitals and religious associations

J.J.C. FOUNDATION, INC.
One Carney Road
West Hartford, CT 06110
(203) 246-6531

Contact Person: Miss Grace Carney
Geographic Giving Pattern: Primarily local
Special Interest: Emphasis on church support - all denominations.
  Also higher education, health agencies and community funds

SULLIVAN (RAY H. AND PAULINE) FOUNDATION
c/o Hartford National Bank & Trust Co.
777 Main Street
Hartford, CT 06115
(203) 728-2703

Contact Person: Hartford National Bank & Trust
Geographic Giving Pattern: Diocese of Norwich, Connecticut
Special Interest: Roman Catholic charities and educational
  institutions

Delaware

LAFFEY-MCHUGH FOUNDATION
919 Market Street
P.O. Box 2207
Wilmington, DE 19899
(302) 658-9141

Contact Person: Arthur G. Connolly, President
Geographic Giving Pattern: Primarily local
Special Interest: Roman Catholic church support and church-related
  institutions

RASKOB FOUNDATION FOR CATHOLIC ACTIVITIES, INC.
P.O. Box 4019
Wilmington, DE 19807
(302) 655-4440

Contact Person: Gerard S. Garey, Executive Director
Geographic Giving Pattern: National, international
Special Interest: Institutions and organizations identified with the
  Roman Catholic church

District of Columbia

DELMAR (THE CHARLES) FOUNDATION
c/o John H. Doyle
918 Sixteenth Street, N.W., Suite 203
Washington, D.C. 20006
(202) 393-2266; (202) 293-2494

Contact Person: John H. Doyle
Geographic Giving Pattern: Washington, D.C., Puerto Rico,
  Latin America
Special Interest: Roman Catholic and Episcopal churches, hospitals,
  welfare organizations

LOUGHRAN (MARY AND DANIEL) FOUNDATION, INC.
c/o American Security & Trust
15th Street & Pennsylvania Ave., N.W.
Washington, D.C. 20013
(202) 624-4283

Contact Person: Roberta Stearns, Assistant Administrator
Geographic Giving Pattern: Washington, D.C., Virginia, Maryland
Special Interest: Religious institutions, youth and social agencies,
  higher education

LOYOLA FOUNDATION, INC., THE
c/o Albert G. McCarthy III
305 C Street, N.E.
Washington, D.C. 20002
(202) 546-9400

Contact Person: Albert G. McCarthy III, Secretary
Geographic Giving Pattern: National, international
Special Interest: Roman Catholic missionary work and other
    Catholic activities of interest to the trustees

Florida

KOCH FOUNDATION, INC.
625-B N.W. 60th Street
Gainesville, FL 32607
(904) 373-7491

Contact Person: Carolyn L. Bomberger, President
Geographic Giving Pattern: National
Special Interest: Roman Catholic religious organizations that
    propagate the faith

LEWIS (FRANK J.) FOUNDATION
P.O. Box 9726
Riviera Beach, FL 33404

Contact Person: Edward D. Lewis, President
Geographic Giving Pattern: National
Special Interest: To foster, preserve and extend the Roman Catholic
    faith. Educational institutions, church support, religious orders,
    church-sponsored programs

Georgia

ST. JOSEPH FOUNDATION, INC.
82 Kennedy Drive
P.O. Box 587
Forest Park, GA 30050

Contact Person: William A. Chesney
Special Interest: Roman Catholic churches and religious
    organizations

Hawaii

HO (CHINN) FOUNDATION
239 Merchant Street
P.O. Box 2668
Honolulu, HI 96803
(808) 537-3891

Contact Person: Donald M. Wong, Treasurer
Geographic Giving Pattern: National
Special Interest: Higher education, Roman Catholic church support

Illinois

BOWYER (THE AMBROSE AND GLADYS) FOUNDATION
135 S. La Salle Street, Suite 1500
Chicago, IL 60603
(312) 346-1030

Contact Person: D.T. Hutchison, President
Geographic Giving Pattern: National
Special Interest: Higher education, hospitals, welfare funds, Roman
   Catholic and Protestant religious organizations

CHRISTIANA FOUNDATION, INC.
69 W. Washington Street, Room 2700
Chicago, IL 60602
(312) 630-4400

Contact Person: Jerome A. Frazel, Jr., President
Geographic Giving Pattern: Primarily local
Special Interest: Roman Catholic community welfare organizations,
   secondary and higher education

CUNEO FOUNDATION, THE
2 N. Riverside Plaza, Suite 1160
Chicago, IL 60606
(312) 648-5100

Contact Person: John F. Cuneo Jr., President
Geographic Giving Pattern: Primarily local
Special Interest: Roman Catholic religious associations, higher
   education and welfare funds

FITZGERALD (FATHER JAMES M.) SCHOLARSHIP TRUST
c/o Commercial National Bank of Peoria
301 S.W. Adams Street
Peoria, IL 61631
(309) 655-5536

Contact Person: Rev. Francis Cahill
Geographic Giving Pattern: Illinois
Special Interest: Scholarships restricted to Illinois residents who are
    studying for the priesthood and attend a Catholic university
    or college

GALVIN (ROBERT W.) FOUNDATION
1303 E. Algonquin Road
Schaumburg, IL 60196
(312) 576-5300

Contact Person: Robert W. Galvin, President
Geographic Giving Pattern: Primarily local
Special Interest: Higher education, aid to the handicapped,
    hospitals, church support and religious organizations

JOYCE (THE JOHN M. AND MARY A.) FOUNDATION
777 Joyce Road
Joliet, IL 60436
(815) 741-7733

Contact Person: William J. Davito, Secretary
Geographic Giving Pattern: National
Special Interest: Roman Catholic churches and religious societies

MAZZA FOUNDATION
400 West Superior Street
Chicago, IL 60610
(312) 787-9893

Contact Person: Neil Vernasco, Assistant Secretary
Geographic Giving Pattern: Chicago
Special Interest: Churches, religious organizations, social agencies,
    Roman Catholic schools of theology

SCHMITT (ARTHUR J.) FOUNDATION
Two North La Salle Street, Suite 2010
Chicago, IL 60602
(312) 236-5089

Contact Person: John A. Donohue, Executive Secretary
Geographic Giving Pattern: Primarily local
Special Interest: Roman Catholic educational and religious
    institutions

SIRAGUSA FOUNDATION, THE
424 E. Howard Avenue
Des Plaines, IL 60018
(312) 827-0033

Contact Person: Melvin T. Tracht, Treasurer
Geographic Giving Pattern: Primarily Mid-west
Special Interest: Roman Catholic with some giving to Protestant
churches, an Eastern Orthodox church and a synagogue

SNITE (FRED B.) FOUNDATION
4800 North Western Avenue
Chicago, IL 60625

Contact Person: Nicholas Rassas, Director
Geographic Giving Pattern: Primarily local
Special Interest: Roman Catholic church support and church-related
educational institutions

SULLIVAN (BOLTON) FUND
One Northfield Plaza, Suite 310
Northfield, IL 60093
(312) 446-1500

Contact Person: Bolton Sullivan, President
Geographic Giving Pattern: National
Special Interest: Roman Catholic church support, secondary and
higher education, church-related institutions and hospitals

WHITE (W.P. AND H.B.) FOUNDATION
2215 Sanders Road, Suite 450
Northbrook, IL 60062
(312) 480-9300

Contact Person: John H. McCortney, Vice-President
Geographic Giving Pattern: Primarily metropolitan Chicago
Special Interest: Roman Catholic church support, higher education,
hospitals, church-related institutions

Louisiana

LIBBY-DUFOUR FUND
P.O. Box 61540
New Orleans, LA 70160
OR 321 Hibernia Bank Building
New Orleans, LA 70112
(504) 586-5552

Contact Person: James A. Stouse, President
Geographic Giving Pattern: Primarily local
Special Interest: Religious education

Maryland

KNOTT (THE MARION I. AND HENRY J.) FOUNDATION, INC.
Two West University Parkway
Baltimore, MD 21218
(301) 727-7733
Application Address
13008 Heil Manor Rd., Route 1, Resistertown, MD 21136
Contact Person: Rose Marie K. Porter
Geographic Giving Pattern: Primarily local
Special Interest: Roman Catholic higher and secondary education, and
religious welfare organizations

MULLAN (THE THOMAS F. AND CLEMANTINE L.)
FOUNDATION, INC.
15 Charles Plaza, Suite 400
Baltimore, MD 21201
(301) 727-6300
Contact Person: Thomas F. Mullan, Jr.
Geographic Giving Pattern: Primarily local
Special Interest: Church support, charitable institutions, higher and
secondary education

Massachusetts

BIRMINGHAM FOUNDATION
c/o Paul Mark Ryan
28 State Street, Suite 3780
Boston, MA 02109
(617) 723-7430
Contact Person: Paul Mark Ryan, Trustee
Geographic Giving Pattern: Primarily local
Special Interest: Roman Catholic charities, education and
church support

WALSH (BLANCHE M.) CHARITY TRUST
c/o John E. Leggat
174 Central Street, Suite 329
Lowell, MA 01852
(617) 454-5654
Contact Person: John E. Leggat, Esq.
Geographic Giving Pattern: National
Special Interest: Roman Catholic charities and education

Michigan

SAGE FOUNDATION
2500 Commercial Building
Detroit, MI 48226
(313) 963-6420
Contact Person: Emmett E. Eagan, Sr., Vice-President
Geographic Giving Pattern: No restrictions
Special Interest: To further charitable, religious, scientific, literary
and educational purposes

SEYMOUR AND TROESTER FOUNDATION
21500 Harper Avenue
St. Clair Shores, MI 48080
(313) 777-2775
Contact Person: B.A. Seymour, Jr., President
Geographic Giving Pattern: National
Special Interest: Roman Catholic charitable and religious
organizations, higher and secondary educational institutions

TRACY (EMMET AND FRANCES) FUND
400 Renaissance Center, 35th Floor
Detroit, MI 48243
(313) 881-5007
Contact Person: Emmet E. Tracy, President
Geographic Giving Pattern: Primarily Michigan, some national
Special Interest: Roman Catholic religious organizations and
missionary groups, hospitals, education

Minnesota

BUTLER (PATRICK AND AIMEE) FAMILY FOUNDATION
W-1380 First National Bank Building
St. Paul, MN 55101
(612) 222-2565
Contact Person: Peter M. Butler, Vice-President
Geographic Giving Pattern: Primarily local
Special Interest: Roman Catholic church and related institutions

KASAL (FATHER) CHARITABLE FUND
c/o Minnesota Trust Company
107 W. Oakland Avenue
Austin, MN 55912
(507) 437-3231

Contact Person: Warren F. Plunkett, President
Geographic Giving Pattern: International
Special Interest: Support for Roman Catholic charities in the
  United States and for the education of young men and women
  for religious life, and mission work

O'NEIL (THE ALBERT T.) FOUNDATION
c/o The American National Bank & Trust Co.
5th and Minnesota
St. Paul, MN 55101
(612) 298-6173

Contact Person: American National Bank & Trust Co.
Geographic Giving Pattern: Primarily local
Special Interest: Roman Catholic religious organizations and
  missions

O'SHAUGHNESSY (I.A.) FOUNDATION
W-555 First National Bank Building
St. Paul, MN 55101
(612) 222-2323

Contact Person: Paul J. Kelly
Geographic Giving Pattern: Primarily Minnesota, Kansas, Texas and
  Illinois
Special Interest: Roman Catholic church-related institutions and
  church support

QUINLAN (THE ELIZABETH C.) FOUNDATION
417 Minnesota Federal Building
Minneapolis, MN 55402
(612) 333-8084

Contact Person: Richard A. Klein, President
Geographic Giving Pattern: Primarily local
Special Interest: Roman Catholic institutions

RAUENHORST (GERALD) FAMILY FOUNDATION
1500 First Bank Plaza W.
Minneapolis, MN 55402
(612) 333-1133

Contact Person: Terence W. Glarner, Vice-President, Managing
  Director
Geographic Giving Pattern: Minnesota
Special Interest: General purpose contributions to well-established,
  religious, educational, and charitable organizations which are
  publicly supported

Missouri

ENRIGHT FOUNDATION, INC.
7508 Main
Kansas City, MO 64114
(816) 361-4942

Contact Person: Anna M. Cassidy
Geographic Giving Pattern: Primarily local
Special Interest: Roman Catholic religious organizations

SYCAMORE TREE TRUST
P.O. Box 11264
Clayton, MO 63105

Contact Person: R.J. Connors, Trustee
Geographic Giving Pattern: Missouri, New York
Special Interest: Roman Catholic church support and religious
  associations

VATTEROTT FOUNDATION
10449 St. Charles Rock Road
St. Ann, MO 63074
(314) 427-4000

Contact Person: Joseph H. Vatterott
Geographic Giving Pattern: Primarily local
Special Interest: Roman Catholic church support and church-related
  institutions

New Jersey

ENGELHARD (THE CHARLES) FOUNDATION
P.O. Box 427
Far Hills, NJ 07931
(201) 766-7224

Contact Person: Elaine Catterall, Secretary
Geographic Giving Pattern: National
Special Interest: Higher and secondary education, religious, cultural,
  medical and conservation organizations

GRASSMANN (E.J.) TRUST
P.O. Box 1088
Elizabeth, NJ 07207
(201) 354-5525

Contact Person: William V. Engel, Executive Director
Geographic Giving Pattern: National
Special Interest: Hospitals, higher education and Roman Catholic
  church support

HACKETT FOUNDATION, INC., THE
2124 Oak Tree Road
Edison, NJ 08820
(201) 548-3686

Contact Person: Denis P. Hackett, President
Special Interest: Roman Catholic religious orders and agencies relating to health and social services in the Northeast and foreign missions

KENNEDY (THE JOHN R.) FOUNDATION, INC.
75 Chestnut Ridge Road
Montvale, NJ 07645
(201) 391-1776

Contact Person: John R. Kennedy, Sr., President
Geographic Giving Pattern: New Jersey, New York, Washington, D.C.
Special Interest: Roman Catholic educational, religious and welfare programs

New York

BRENCANDA FOUNDATION
358 Fifth Avenue, Suite 900
New York, NY 10001

Contact Person: Peter S. Robinson, Executive Vice-President
Geographic Giving Pattern: United States and Canada
Special Interest: Roman Catholic religious organizations

GAISMAN (THE CATHERINE AND HENRY J.) FOUNDATION
Box 277
Hartsdale, NY 10530

Contact Person: Catherine V. Gaisman, President
Geographic Giving Pattern: Primarily local
Special Interest: Roman Catholic church suport

HOMELAND FOUNDATION
c/o Kelley, Drye and Warren
350 Park Avenue
New York, NY 10022
(212) 808-7803

Contact Person: Louis B. Warren, Trustee
Geographic Giving Pattern: National, international

HOPKINS (JOSEPHINE LAWRENCE) FOUNDATION
61 Broadway, Room 2912
New York, NY 10006
(212) 480-0400

Contact Person: Ivan Obolensky, President and Treasurer
Geographic Giving Pattern: Primarily local
Special Interest: Roman Catholic church support. Also hospitals
  and medical research, community funds and cultural programs

LA SALA (THE STEFANO) FOUNDATION, INC.
371 North Avenue
New Rochelle, NY 10801
(914) 235-1974

Contact Person: Frank La Sala, Trustee
Geographic Giving Pattern: Primarily local
Special Interest: Church support, education, missions

MASTRONARDI (THE CHARLES A.) FOUNDATION
c/o Morgan Guaranty Trust Company
9 West 57th Street
New York, NY 10019
(212) 826-7603

Contact Person: Edward F. Bennett, Vice-President
Geographic Giving Pattern: Primarily New York and Florida
Special Interest: Higher education, child welfare, hospitals, Roman
  Catholic church support

MCCADDIN-MCQUIRK FOUNDATION, INC., THE
1002 Madison Avenue
New York, NY 10021
(212) 772-9090

Contact Person: Robert W. Dumser, Secretary
Geographic Giving Pattern: International
Special Interest: "Foster educational opportunities for poorer
  students to be priests, deacons, catechists or lay teachers of the
  Roman Catholic church. . . ." Application must be submitted by
  a Bishop, Rector, or head of a seminary

MCCARTHY CHARITIES, INC., THE
P.O. Box 576
Troy, NY 12181

Contact Person: James A. McCarthy, Vice-President
Geographic Giving Pattern: Primarily local
Special Interest: Roman Catholic church support, church-related
  education and welfare agencies

MCCARTHY (THE MICHAEL W.) FOUNDATION
One Liberty Plaza, 27th Floor
New York, NY 10006

Contact Person: Michael W. McCarthy, Manager
Geographic Giving Pattern: National
Special Interest: Higher education, Church support and religious
  associations

MORANIA FOUNDATION, INC.
c/o Morgan Trust Company
9 West 57th Street
New York, NY 10019
(212) 826-7255

Contact Person: William J. McCormack, President
Geographic Giving Pattern: Primarily New York, some New
  England
Special Interest: Roman Catholic church-related institutions with
  emphasis on missions

O'NEIL (CYRIL F. AND MARIE E.) FOUNDATION
c/o Richards, O'Neil & Allegaert
660 Madison Avenue
New York, NY 10021
(212) 759-2020

Contact Person: Ralph M. O'Neil, President
Geographic Giving Pattern: Primarily local, some national
Special Interest: Education and Catholic religious organizations

O'TOOLE (THERESA AND EDWARD) FOUNDATION
c/o The Bank of New York
48 Wall Street
New York, NY 10015

Contact Person: Chris Degheri, Trustee
Special Interest: Roman Catholic welfare and educational funds

POPE FOUNDATION, THE
1740 Broadway
New York, NY 10019

Contact Person: Fortune Pope, Vice-President
Geographic Giving Pattern: Primarily local, some national and
  international
Special Interest: Education, religion, relief and rehabilitation,
  hospitals, and medical research. Also civic organizations

74

NK (A.J.) FAMILY *FOUNDATION*
Box 1467
City, OR 97360
act Person: A.J. Frank, President
raphic Giving Pattern: Primarily local
al Interest: Roman Catholic church support and welfare funds

N (B.P.) *FOUNDATION*
Standard Plaza
and, OR 97204
tact Person: Lester M. John, President, Treasurer
graphic Giving Pattern: National, international
ial Interest: Roman Catholic religious, charitable and
ucational organizations

N (HELEN) *FOUNDATION*
Standard Plaza
and, OR 97204
tact Person: James G. Condon, President
graphic Giving Pattern: Primarily local
ial Interest: Roman Catholic religious, charitable, educational
rposes

ylvania

NNELLY FOUNDATION
) Ashton Road
adelphia, PA 19136
) 698-5203
ntact Person: John F. Connelly, President
graphic Giving Pattern: Primarily Philadelphia area
cial Interest: Religious and educational institutions and hospitals

NNELLY (MARY J.) FOUNDATION
Thomas J. Donnelly
) Centre City Tower
sburgh, PA 15222
) 471-5828
ntact Person: Thomas J. Donnelly, Trustee
graphic Giving Pattern: Primarily local, some New York, West
irginia, North Carolina, Washington, D.C. and Connecticut
cial Interest: Roman Catholic educational, welfare, and religious
rganizations

REISS (JACOB L.) FOUNDATION
c/o Irving Trust Company
P.O. Box 12446
Church Street Station
New York, NY 10249

Contact Person: Irving Trust Co., Trustee
Geographic Giving Pattern: Primarily New York, New Jersey,
  Wisconsin
Special Interest: Hospitals, Roman Catholic educational and welfare
  organizations

SAYOUR (ELIAS) FOUNDATION, INC.
185 Madison Avenue
New York, NY 10016
(212) 686-7560

Contact Person: Jeanette Sayour, President
Geographic Giving Pattern: Primarily local
Special Interest: Roman Catholic church support, welfare funds,
  educational and religious organizations

VOLLMER FOUNDATION, INC.
c/o Aragua Services, Inc.
745 Fifth Avenue
New York, NY 10022
(212) 752-0969

Contact Person: Albert L. Ennist, Assistant Secretary
Geographic Giving Pattern: International
Special Interest: Charitable, scientific and educational activities
  which will benefit the people of Venezuela, Latin America and
  the Catholic Church. Also support for international youth
  organizations

WALTERS FAMILY FOUNDATION, INC.
548 Manhasset Woods Road
Manhasset, NY 11030
(516) 627-0908

Contact Person: Bernard F. Walters, President
Geographic Giving Pattern: Local
Special Interest: Roman Catholic church support

North Carolina

BRYAN (THE KATHLEEN PRICE AND JOSEPH M.) FAMILY
  FOUNDATION
P.O. Box 21008
Greensboro, NC 27420
(919) 378-2242

Contact Person: Allan M. Herrick, Associate
Geographic Giving Pattern: Primarily North Carolina
Special Interest: Religious and educational institutions

Ohio

AHS FOUNDATION
909 East Ohio Building
Cleveland, OH 44114
(216) 621-5578

Contact Person: c/o John L. Jerry; First Trust Co. of St. Paul,
  W-555 First National Bank Building, St. Paul, MN 55101
Geographic Giving Pattern: Primarily local
Special Interest: Roman Catholic church support

BENTZ FOUNDATION
2569 Berwick Blvd.
Columbus, OH 43209
(614) 239-0920

Contact Person: George B. Bentz, President
Geographic Giving Pattern: National, international
Special Interest: Missions, church support

KUNTZ FOUNDATION
120 West Second Street
Dayton, OH 45402
(513) 461-3870

Contact Person: Peter H. Kuntz, President
Geographic Giving Pattern: Primarily local
Special Interest: Higher education, hospitals, community funds,
  Roman Catholic church and missions support

LENNON (FRED A.) FOUNDATION
29500 Solon Road
Solon, OH 44139
(216) 248-4600

Contact Person: John F. Fant, Jr., Secretary
Geographic Giving Pattern: Primarily local
Special Interest: Higher education, hospitals,
  Roman Catholic church support

O'NEIL (THE W.) FOUNDATION
One General Street
Akron, OH 44329
(216) 666-6006

Contact Person: Miss Flora Flint, Vice-Preside
  Secretary-Treasurer
Geographic Giving Pattern: National
Special Interest: Roman Catholic church supp
  institutions

O'NEILL BROTHERS FOUNDATION, THE
23200 Chagrin Blvd.
Cleveland, OH 44122
(216) 464-2121

Contact Person: Patrick O'Neill, President
Geographic Giving Pattern: Cleveland, Ohio an
Special Interest: Roman Catholic religious orgar
  church support

Oklahoma

WARREN (THE WILLIAM K.) FOUNDATION
P.O. Box 45372
Tulsa, OK 74145
(918) 492-8100

Contact Person: C.J. Senger, President
Geographic Giving Pattern: National
Special Interest: Church support, Roman Catholi
  associations, local medical research centers and

Oregon

CLARK FOUNDATION
200 Market Building, Suite 350
Portland, OR 97201
(503) 223-5290

Contact Person: Maurie D. Clark, President
Geographic Giving Pattern: Oregon
Special Interest: Roman Catholic educational, religic
  medical organizations

KELLEY (KATE M.) FOUNDATION
301 Meade Street
Pittsburgh, PA 15221
(412) 243-3080
Contact Person: Edward C. Ifft, Trustee
Geographic Giving Pattern: National
Special Interest: Roman Catholic church, education, welfare support

MCSHAIN (JOHN) CHARITIES
540 N. 17th Street
Philadelphia, PA 19130
(215) 564-2322
Contact Person: John McShain, President
Geographic Giving Pattern: Primarily local
Special Interest: Roman Catholic religious, educational and welfare
  purposes

ST. MARYS CATHOLIC FOUNDATION
1935 State Street
St. Marys, PA 15857
Contact Person: Richard J. Reuscher, Secretary-Treasurer
Geographic Giving Pattern: Pennsylvania, New Jersey, Indiana,
  New York, Washington, D.C.
Special Interest: Roman Catholic schools - all levels. Also religious
  associations

Texas

BURKITT FOUNDATION, THE
2000 West Loop South, Suite 1485
Houston, TX 77027
(713) 439-0149
Contact Person: Cornelius O. Ryan, President
Geographic Giving Pattern: Primarily local, some national,
  international
Special Interest: Roman Catholic church-sponsored programs

CAMERON (HARRY S. AND ISABEL C.) FOUNDATION
P.O. Box 2555
Houston, TX 77001
(713) 652-6526
Contact Person: Carl W. Schumacher, Jr.
Geographic Giving Pattern: Primarily local, some national
Special Interest: Roman Catholic churches, schools - all levels, and
  religious organizations

DOUGHERTY (THE JAMES R.) JR. FOUNDATION
P.O. Box 640
Beeville, TX 78102
(512) 358-3560

Contact Person: Hugh Grove, Jr., Assistant Secretary
Geographic Giving Pattern: Primarily local
Special Interest: Roman Catholic church-related institutions

HENCK (AUGUST J. AND SADIE L.) MEMORIAL FUND
P.O. Box 1237
Austin, TX 78767
(512) 477-9831

Contact Person: Henck Memorial Fund Trustees
Geographic Giving Pattern: Primarily Texas
Special Interest: Roman Catholic organizations

STRAKE FOUNDATION
3300 Gulf Building
Houston, TX 77002
(713) 227-2065

Contact Person: George W. Strake, Jr., President
Geographic Giving Pattern: National with emphasis on Texas
Special Interest: Public charitable, religious, educational, scientific
and/or literary purposes for the public good

Washington

NORCLIFFE FUND, THE
1001 Fourth Avenue
Seattle, WA 98154
(206) 682-4820

Contact Person: Mrs. Mary Hurd, Manager
Geographic Giving Pattern: Pacific Northwest
Special Interest: Church support, religious associations, education,
youth, aged

Wisconsin

DE RANCE, INC.
7700 West Blue Mound Road
Milwaukee, WI 53213
(414) 475-7700

Contact Person: Harry G. John, President
Geographic Giving Pattern: National, international
Special Interest: Roman Catholic church support, religious
associations, missionary work, welfare

Jewish Foundations

California

AMADO (MAURICE) FOUNDATION
1800 Century Park East, Suite 200
Los Angeles, CA 90067
(213) 556-0116
Contact Person: Richard J. Amado, President
Special Interest: Sephardic Jewish causes

FRIEDMAN BROTHERS FOUNDATION
801 E. Commercial Street
Los Angeles, CA 90012
Contact Person: William Borenstein, Trustee
Geographic Giving Pattern: Primarily local
Special Interest: Education, including religious education and Jewish welfare funds

G.A.G. CHARITABLE CORPORATION
P.O. Box 42
Badger, CA 93603
(209) 337-2885
Contact Person: Dorothy Salant Garrett,President
Geographic Giving Pattern: New York and California
Special Interest: Religious organizations and Jewish welfare funds

HAAS (WALTER AND ELISE) FUND
1155 Battery Street
San Francisco, CA 94111
(415) 986-5177
Contact Person: Sanford H. Treguboff
Geographic Giving Pattern: Israel and California
Special Interest: Jewish religious purposes

LEVY (HYMAN JEBB) FOUNDATION
2222 S. Figueroa Street
Los Angeles, CA 90007
(213) 749-9441
Contact Person: Hyman J. Levy, President
Geographic Giving Pattern: United States and Israel
Special Interest: Jewish education and temple support

LOWY FAMILY FOUNDATION
P.O. Box 5526
Beverly Hills, CA 90210

Contact Person: Marcus Lowy, President
Geographic Giving Pattern: Primarily local
Special Interest: Jewish organizations and temple support

NEWMAN (CALVIN M. AND RACQUEL) CHARITABLE
TRUST
27500 La Vida Real
Los Altos Hills, CA 94022

Contact Person: Racquel H. Naymark, Trustee
Geographic Giving Pattern: Primarily local
Special Interest: Jewish welfare funds, religious education

NEWHOUSE FOUNDATION, INC.
220 Bush Street, Suite 1821
San Francisco, CA 94104
(415) 986-5182

Contact Person: Sanford M. Treguboff
Geographic Giving Pattern: San Francisco Bay area
Special Interest: Jewish charities and through these to needy
  individuals of the Jewish race and/or religion

SHAPELL (DAVID AND FELA) FOUNDATION
9402 Wilshire Blvd., Suite 770
Beverly Hills, CA 90212
(213) 273-7337

Contact Person: David Shapell, President
Geographic Giving Pattern: California, New York and Israel
Special Interest: Jewish welfare funds, temple support, religious
  education

WEINBERG (ADOLPH AND ETTA) FOUNDATION
12948 S. Pioneer Blvd.
P.O. Box 723
Norwalk, CA 90650
(213) 864-2781

Contact Person: Ray Molene
Geographic Giving Pattern: Primarily local
Special Interest: Jewish religious organizations and temple support

Colorado

COORS (ADOLPH) FOUNDATION
350 - C Clayton Street
Denver, CO 80206
(303) 388-1636

Contact Person: Gordon C. Jones, Executive Manager
Geographic Giving Pattern: Primarily Colorado
Special Interest: To support religious, charitable and educational
   organizations - Jewish or Christian

Delaware

KUTZ (MILTON AND HATTIE) FOUNDATION
101 Garden of Eden Road
Wilmington, DE 19803
(302) 478-6200

Contact Person: Morris Lapidos, Executive Secretary
Geographic Giving Pattern: Local
Special Interest: Jewish religious organizations and temple support

District of Columbia

*GUDELSKY (THE ISADORE AND BERTHA) FAMILY
   FOUNDATION, INC.*
c/o Philip Margolius
1503 21st street, N.W.
Washington, D.C. 20036
(202) 328-0500

Contact Person: Philip Margolius
Geographic Giving Pattern: Primarily local
Special Interest: Jewish welfare funds and temple support

Florida

APPLEBAUM FOUNDATION, INC., THE
4925 Collins Avenue
Miami Beach, FL 33140
(305) 651-6478

Contact Person: Joseph Applebaum
Geographic Giving Pattern: General
Special Interest: Higher education, hospitals, medical research,
   Jewish welfare agencies, religious schools and temple support

BLANK (SAMUEL AND FAMILY) FOUNDATION
11077 N.W. 36th Avenue
P.O. Box 680310
Miami, FL 33168
(305) 685-3851

Contact Person: Marvin Florman
Geographic Giving Pattern: Primarily local
Special Interest: Jewish welfare funds, hospitals, education,
   temple support

Illinois

PRITZKER FOUNDATION
2 First National Plaza, 30th Floor
Chicago, IL 60603
(312) 621-4200

Contact Person: A.N. Pritzker, President
Geographic Giving Pattern: National
Special Interest: Higher education, religious welfare funds and
   temple support

SHAPIRO (CHARLES AND M.R.) FOUNDATION, INC.
330 W. Diversey Parkway #1801
Chicago, IL 60657

Contact Person: Morris R. Shapiro, President
Geographic Giving Pattern: Primarily local
Special Interest: Jewish welfare, temple support. Also contributions
   to Catholic and Protestant churches

Iowa

ALIBIR FOUNDATION
1200 Carriers Building
Des Moines, IA 50309
(515) 288-9723

Contact Person: Philip Burns, Treasurer
Geographic Giving Pattern: Primarily local
Special Interest: Higher education, Jewish welfare funds, and
   temple support

Maryland

CHERTKOF (DAVID W. AND ANNIE) MITZVAH FUND, INC.
19 W. Franklin Street
Baltimore, MD 21201
(301) 727-5155

Contact Person: Howard L. Chertkof, Secretary
Geographic Giving Pattern: Maryland, New York and Florida
Special Interest: Jewish sponsored educational programs, temples, welfare funds

MENDELSON (AFLRED G. AND IDA) FAMILY FOUNDATION
8300 Pennsylvania Avenue
Forestville, MD 20747-0398

Contact Person: Ida Mendelson, President
Geographic Giving Pattern: Primarily local
Special Interest: Jewish religious organizations. Also community, social services, and educational funds

WASSERMAN (GEORGE) FOUNDATION, INC.
5454 Wisconsin Avenue, Suite 1300
Chevy Chase, MD 20815
(301) 657-4222

Contact Person: Loius C. Grossberg, President and Treasurer
Geographic Giving Pattern: International
Special Interest: Jewish welfare funds, theological studies, temple support

WEINBERG (THE HARRY AND JEANETTE) FOUNDATION, INC.
5518 Baltimore National Pike
Baltimore, MD 21228
(301) 744-6142

Contact Person: Nathan Weinberg, Vice-President and Secretary
Geographic Giving Pattern: Hawaii, Baltimore, Scranton, Pennsylvania
Special Interest: Jewish welfare funds, temple support, higher education

Michigan

BARGMAN (THEODORE AND MINA) FOUNDATION
29201 Telegraph Road, Suite 500
Southfield, MI 48034
(313) 353-9500

Contact Person: Joseph H. Jackier, President
Geographic Giving Pattern: National, international
Special Interest: Primarily religious giving with emphasis on Jewish
welfare funds, higher education in Israel, and temple support

HERMAN (JOHN AND ROSE) FOUNDATION
3001 W. Big Beaver Pond, Suite 404
Troy, MI 48084
(313) 649-6400

Contact Person: Harold S. Tobias, Secretary
Geographic Giving Pattern: Primarily local
Special Interest: Jewish welfare funds and temple support

NUSBAUM (SOL) FAMILY FOUNDATION
17116 Jeanette
Southfield, MI 48075
(313) 557-2653

Contact Person: Joseph Nusbaum, President
Geographic Giving Pattern: Local, Michigan and New York City
Special Interest: Rabbinical training, temple support, welfare

PRENTIS (THE MEYER AND ANNA) FAMILY FOUNDATION, INC.
14500 W. Seven Mile Road
Detroit, MI 48235
(313) 342-7100

Contact Person: Lester Morris, Secretary
Geographic Giving Pattern: National
Special Interest: Temple support, education, health and welfare
organizations

STOLLMAN FOUNDATION, THE
2900 W. Maple Road
Troy, MI 48084
(313) 643-6140

Contact Person: Max Stollman, President
Geographic Giving Pattern: New York, Michigan and Israel
Special Interest: Religious education, temple support, welfare funds

Minnesota

PHILLIPS FOUNDATION, THE
Midwest Plaza, West Building
Minneapolis, MN 55402
(612) 331-6230

Contact Person: Thomas P. Cook, Executive Director
Geographic Giving Pattern: Primarily mid-west
Special Interest: Higher education including medical and theological, Jewish welfare and temple support

Nebraska

LIVINGSTON (THE MILTON S. AND CORINNE N.) FOUNDATION, INC.
300 Overland Wolf Center
6910 Pacific Street
Omaha, NE 68106
(402) 558-1112

Contact Person: Yale Richards, Secretary
Geographic Giving Pattern: Primarily local
Special Interest: Jewish welfare funds, higher education, temple support

New Jersey

FRISCH FOUNDATION, INC., THE
1600 Parker Avenue
Fort Lee, NJ 07024
(212) 324-0300
Mailing Address: 501 East 79th St., New York, NY 10021

Contact Person: Alfred M. Frisch, President
Geographic Giving Pattern: United States and Israel
Special Interest: Jewish welfare funds, temple support. Also higher education, women's organizations and hospitals

ROSENHAUS (THE SARAH AND MATTHEW) PEACE FOUNDATION, INC.
Picatinny Road
Morristown, NJ 07960
(201) 267-6583

Contact Person: Irving Rosenhaus, Director
Geographic Giving Pattern: Primarily New Jersey and New York
Special Interest: To promote world peace and understanding. Grants to higher education including theological. Also to Jewish welfare funds and temple support

New York

ADES FOUNDATION, INC
17 E. 37th Street
New York, NY 10016

Contact Person: Joseph Ades, President
Geographic Giving Pattern: New York and Israel
Special Interest: Jewish welfare, temple support, education

BENDHEIM (CHARLES AND ELS) FOUNDATION
10 Columbus Circle
New York, NY 10019

Contact Person: Charles H. Bendheim, President
Geographic Giving Pattern: National
Special Interest: Jewish sponsored religious and educational
  institutions and welfare funds

BRAND (THE MARTHA AND REGINA) FOUNDATION, INC.
150 Broadway
New York, NY 10038
(212) 227-8500

Contact Person: Nathan B. Kogan, President
Geographic Giving Pattern: Primarily local
Special Interest: Jewish welfare funds, temple support, and a
  theological seminary

DANIEL (GERARD AND RUTH) FOUNDATION, INC.
5 Plain Avenue
New Rochelle, NY 10801
(914) 235-2525

Contact Person: Gerard Daniel, President
Geographic Giving Pattern: Primarily local
Special Interest: Jewish religious and welfare funds

DAVIS (SIMON AND ANNA) FOUNDATION
c/o Davis & Gilbert
850 Third Avenue
New York, NY 10022
(212) 593-0707

Contact Person: Paul B. Gibney, Jr., President and Treasurer
Geographic Giving Pattern: Primarily local
Special Interest: Religious welfare funds, higher education in the
  United States and Israel

GOLDSTEIN (SAMUEL AND ABRAHAM) FOUNDATION
7600 Jericho Turnpike
Woodbury, NY 11797
(516) 364-2800

Contact Person: Abraham Goldstein, Trustee
Geographic Giving Pattern: New York and Israel
Special Interest: Religious institutions, welfare, higher education

HASENFELD (A. AND Z.) FOUNDATION, INC.
580 Fifth Avenue
New York, NY 10036

Contact Person: Alexander Hasenfeld, President
Special Interest: Jewish welfare funds, temple support

HESS FOUNDATION, INC.
1185 Avenue of the Americas
New York, NY 10036
(212) 997-8500

Contact Person: Leon Hess, President
Geographic Giving Pattern: National
Special Interest: A disaster relief fund, education, temple and
   church support

JESSELSON FOUNDATION
1221 Avenue of the Americas
New York, NY 10020

Contact Person: Ludwig Jesselson, President and Treasurer
Geographic Giving Pattern: International
Special Interest: Temple support, Jewish welfare funds, Jewish-
   sponsored educational and charitable institutions

MORGANSTERN (MORRIS) FOUNDATION
100 Merrick Road
Rockville Center, NY 11570
(516) 536-3030

Contact Person: Hannah Klein, Executive Director
Geographic Giving Pattern: Primarily New York area
Special Interest: Jewish welfare funds, religious institutions,
   particularly synagogues

OVERSEAS FOUNDATIONS, INC.
511 Fifth Avenue
New York, NY 10017
(212) 578-1690

Contact Person: Morton P. Hyman, Manager
Geographic Giving Pattern: National, primarily New York.
 Also Israel
Special Interest: Charitable, educational, religious

RAMAPO TRUST
100 E. 42nd Street, Room 1020
New York, NY 10017
(212) 867-8600
Contact Person: Stephen L. Schwartz, Manager
Geographic Giving Pattern: Primarily New York, New Jersey
Special Interest: Charitable, religious, educational purposes

RIDGEFIELD FOUNDATION, THE
820 Second Avenue
New York, NY 10017
212-692-9570
Contact Person: Louis J. Lipton, Manager
Geographic Giving Pattern: National, also Israel
Special Interest: Charitable, religious, educational purposes

STEIN (JOSEPH F.) FOUNDATION, INC.
28 Aspen Road
Scarsdale, NY 10583
(914) 725-1770
Contact Person: Melvin M. Stein, Manager
Geographic Giving Pattern: Primarily local
Special Interest: Religious education and Jewish welfare

STERN (JEROME L. AND JANE) FOUNDATION, INC.
745 Fifth Avenue
New York, NY 10022
Contact Person: Jerome L. Stern, Chairman
Geographic Giving Pattern: Primarily local
Special Interest: Jewish religious education, temple support and
 Jewish welfare funds

TANANBAUM (MARTIN) FOUNDATION, INC.
261 Madison Avenue, 16th Floor
New York, NY 10017
(212) 687-3440
Contact Person: Arnold S. Alperstein, Manager
Geographic Giving Pattern: National
Special Interest: Religious education, temple support, welfare

TUDOR FOUNDATION, INC.
551 Fifth Avenue
New York, NY 10176
(212) 682-8490

Contact Person: Edwin A. Malloy, Treasurer
Geographic Giving Pattern: National
Special Interest: "To promote a better understanding among peoples
   of all races, creeds and backgrounds." Grants to institutions
   promoting this purpose. Support also for Jewish theological
   education and welfare

WOLFKOWSKI FOUNDATION, INC.
One State Street Plaza
New York, NY 10004

Contact Person: Abraham Wolfson, Manager
Geographic Giving Pattern: United States and Israel
Special Interest: Jewish religious education, temple support and
   welfare funds

WURZWEILER (THE GUSTAV) FOUNDATION, INC.
129 E. 73rd Street
New York, NY 10021
(212) 744-6400

Contact Person: Fred Grubal, Executive Secretary
Geographic Giving Pattern: United States and Israel
Special Interest: Jewish philanthropic and educational institutions
   with emphasis on Jewish history, religious education and
   temple support

Ohio

MELTON (SAMUEL MENDEL) FOUNDATION
88 East Broad Street, Room 1425
Columbus, OH 43215
(614) 224-5239

Contact Person: Samuel M. Melton
Geographic Giving Pattern: United States and Israel
Special Interest: Higher education and youth agencies in Israel and
   Jewish religious educational organizations

SAPIRSTEIN (THE JACOB) FOUNDATION OF CLEVELAND
10500 Americans Road
Cleveland, OH 44144
(216) 525-7300

Contact Person: Irving R. Stone, President
Geographic Giving Pattern: National
Special Interest: Jewish welfare funds, secondary and higher religious education

Pennsylvania

HYMAN FAMILY FOUNDATION
6315 Forbes Avenue
Pittsburgh, PA 15217
(412) 521-1000
Contact Person: Mrs. Yetta Elinoff, Manager
Geographic Giving Pattern: Primarily local
Special Interest: Temple support, religious education, welfare

KLINE (CHARLES AND FIGA) FOUNDATION
302 Colonial Building
Allentown, PA 18101
(215) 434-6149
Contact Person: Leonard Rapoport, Director
Geographic Giving Pattern: Primarily local
Special Interest: Temple support and Jewish welfare agencies

MILLSTEIN CHARITABLE FOUNDATION, THE
N. 4th Street & Gaskill Avenue
Jeanette, PA 15644
(412) 523-5531
Contact Person: David J. Millstein, Executive Secretary
Special Interest: Jewish welfare funds, temple support

STEINSAPIR (JULIUS L. AND LIBBIE B.) FAMILY FOUNDATION
900 Lawyers Building
Pittsburgh, PA 15219
(412) 391-2920
Contact Person: Samuel Horovitz, Trustee
Geographic Giving Pattern: Primarily local
Special Interest: Temple support, Jewish welfare funds, education

Rhode Island

HASSENFELD FOUNDATION, THE
1027 Newport Avenue
Pawtucket, RI 02861
(401) 726-4100

Contact Person: Stephen Hassenfeld, Secretary-Treasurer
Geographic Giving Pattern: Rhode Island and Jerusalem
Special Interest: Jewish welfare funds, religious organizations, education

Tennessee

BELZ FOUNDATION
5118 Park Avenue
Memphis, TN 38117
(901) 767-4780

Contact Person: Jack A. Belz, Manager
Geographic Giving Pattern: Primarily local
Special Interest: Jewish welfare funds, temple support, education

GOLDSMITH FOUNDATION, INC.
123 S. Main Street
P.O. Box 449
Memphis, TN 38143
(901) 529-4716

Contact Person: Jack L. Goldsmith, President
Geographic Giving Pattern: Primarily local, some national
Special Interest: Charitable, medical, educational, religious including temple support

Wisconsin

KOHL (ALLEN D.) CHARITABLE FOUNDATION, INC.
777 East Wisconsin Avenue, Suite 2340
Milwaukee, WI 53202
(414) 347-2340

Contact Person: Allen D. Kohl, President
Geographic Giving Pattern: Primarily local
Special Interest: Jewish welfare and temple support

Interfaith Foundations

California

CASTLE & COOK INTERNATIONAL CHARITABLE FUND, INC.
50 California Street
San Francisco, CA 94111
(415) 986-3000

Contact Person: D.J. Kirchhoff, President
Geographic Giving Pattern: International, Costa Rica, Honduras, Equador, Phillippines, Nicaragua, Thailand
Special Interest: Education, hospitals, child welfare and church support
Religious Preference: Protestant, Roman Catholic

HEARST FOUNDATION, INC., THE
690 Market Street, Suite 502
San Francisco, CA 94104
(415) 781-8418

Contact Person: Charles L. Gould, Vice-President and Senior Executive for programs headquartered west of the Mississippi River
Geographic Giving Pattern: Within the United States and its possessions
Special Interest: Poverty level and minority groups, education at all levels, health and medical research, cultural and religious programs
Religious Preference: Protestant, Roman Catholic, Jewish

HERBST FOUNDATION, INC., THE
4 Embarcadero Center
San Francisco, CA 94111
(415) 398-1212

Contact Person: John T. Seigle, Manager
Geographic Giving Pattern: Primarily local
Special Interest: Educational and religious organizations
Religious Preference: Protestant, Roman Catholic, Jewish

JEWETT (GEORGE FREDERICK) FOUNDATION
One Maritime Plaza
The Alcoa Building, Suite 1340
San Francisco, CA 94111
(415) 421-1351

Contact Person: Sara C. Fernandez, Program Director
Geographic Giving Pattern: Primarily Pacific Northwest
Special Interest: Religious training
Religious Preference: Protestant, Roman Catholic

District of Columbia

MCGREGOR (THOMAS AND FRANCES) FOUNDATION
c/o Robert Philipson & Co.
2000 L Street, N.W., Suite 609
Washington, D.C. 20036

Contact Person: Victor Krakower; 2102 L St. N.W., Washington, D.C. 20037, (202) 333-4411
Geographic Giving Pattern: Primarily local
Special Interest: Education, hopitals, health agencies, cultural programs and religious organizations - Jewish, Catholic, Protestant

STEUART (GUY T.) FOUNDATION
4646 Fortieth Street, N.W.
Washington, D.C. 20016
(202) 537-8940

Contact Person: Curtis S. Steuart, President
Geographic Giving Pattern: Primarily local
Special Interest: Church support, education, hospitals, youth agencies
Religious Preference: Protestant, Roman Catholic, Jewish

Florida

DAVIS (THE ARTHUR VINING) FOUNDATIONS
Haskell Building, Suite 520
Oak and Fisk Streets
Jacksonville, FL 32204
(904) 359-0670

Contact Person: Dr. Max K. Morris, Executive Director
Geographic Giving Pattern: National
Special Interest: Theological seminaries, campus ministry
Religious Preference: Protestant, Roman Catholic, Jewish

JENKINS (GEORGE W.) FOUNDATION, INC.
P.O. Box 407
Lakeland, FL 33802

Contact Person: George W. Jenkins, President
Geographic Giving Pattern: Primarily local
Special Interest: Church support
Religious Preference: Protestant, Roman Catholic, Jewish

THOMAS (DOROTHY) FOUNDATION, INC.
P.O. Box 3436
Tampa, FL 33601
(813) 229-3222

Contact Person: Michael Thomas, Manager
Geographic Giving Pattern: Florida, Texas
Special Interest: Church and education related activities
Religious Preference: Protestant, Roman Catholic

Illinois

SULZER FAMILY FOUNDATION
1940 West Irving Park Road
Chicago, IL 60613

Contact Person: John J. Hoellen, President
Geographic Giving Pattern: Primarily local
Special Interest: Church support and religous organizations
Religious Preference: Protestant, Roman Catholic, Jewish

Indiana

HILLENBRAND (JOHN A.) FOUNDATION
Highway 46
Batesville, IN 47006
(812) 934-7000

Contact Person: William A. Hillenbrand, President
Geographic Giving Pattern: Primarily Batesville and Ripley
   County, Indiana
Special Interest: Church support
Religious Preference: Protestant, Roman Catholic

IRWIN-SWEENEY-MILLER FOUNDATION
420 Third Street
P.O. Box 808
Columbus, IN 47201
(812) 372-0251

Contact Person: John L. Lewis, Program Officer
Geographic Giving Pattern: Primarily local
Special Interest: Religion, the arts, social justice, education
Religious Preference: Protestant, Roman Catholic, Jewish

LILLY ENDOWMENT, INC.
2801 North Meridian Street
P.O. Box 88068
Indianapolis, IN 46208
(317) 924-5471

Contact Person: Robert Lynn, Vice-President - Religion
Geographic Giving Pattern: National
Special Interest: Theological seminaries, Black church leadership, youth ministry
Religious Preference: Protestant, Roman Catholic, Jewish

Massachusetts

JOHNSON (THE HOWARD) FOUNDATION
One Howard Johnson Plaza
Dorchester, MA 02125
(617) 848-2350
Mailing Address: c/o Howard B. Johnson, 50 Rockefeller Plaza, New York, NY 10020
Contact Person: Eugene J. Burden, Secretary
Geographic Giving Pattern: National
Special Interest: Religious welfare, education, health and church support
Religious Preference: Roman Catholic, Protestant

Michigan

KRESGE FOUNDATION, THE
2401 W. Big Beaver Road
Troy, MI 48084
(313) 643-9630
Contact Person: Alfred H. Taylor, Jr., President
Geographic Giving Pattern: National
Special Interest: Building projects
Religious Preference: Protestant, Roman Catholic, Jewish

McGREGOR FUND
333 West Fort Building, Suite 1380
Detroit, MI 48226
(313) 963-3495
Contact Person: Jack L. Otto, Executive Director
Geographic Giving Pattern: Primarily Detroit metropolitan area and Michigan
Special Interest: Education, humanities and sciences
Religious Preference: Protestant, Roman Catholic, Jewish

Minnesota

RIVERS (MARGARET) FUND
c/o William D. Klapp
First National Bank Building
Stillwater, MN 55082
(612) 439-4411

Contact Person: William D. Klapp, President
Geographic Giving Pattern: Primarily local
Special Interest: Church support
Religious Preference: Protestant, Roman Catholic, Jewish

Missouri

GAYLORD (THE CATHERINE MANLEY) FOUNDATION
314 N. Broadway, Room 1230
St. Louis, MO 63102
(314) 421-0181

Contact Person: Donald E. Fahey, Trustee
Geographic Giving Pattern: Primarily local
Special Interest: Church support, education, child welfare and
    homes for the aged
Religious Preference: Protestant, Roman Catholic

New York

ALTMAN FOUNDATION
361 Fifth Avenue
New York, NY 10016
(212) 679-7800

Contact Person: John S. Burke, Jr., President
Geographic Giving Pattern: New York State
Special Interest: To aid charitable and educational institutions with
    emphasis on religious associations
Religious Preference: Protestant, Roman Catholic, Jewish

BOOTH FERRIS FOUNDATION
30 Broad Street
New York, NY 10004
(212) 269-3850

Contact Person: Robert J. Murtagh, Trustee
Geographic Giving Pattern: National
Special Interest: Theological seminaries
Religious Preference: Protestant, Roman Catholic, Jewish

CLARK (FRANK E.) CHARITABLE TRUST
c/o Manufacturers Hanover Trust Company
600 Fifth Avenue
New York, NY 10020
(212) 957-1426

Contact Person: Helen M. Thome, Vice-President
Geographic Giving Pattern: Primarily local
Special Interest: Charitable and religious purposes. Income is
distributed to the parent body of major religious denominations
for aid to needy churches

COLT (JAMES J.) FOUNDATION, INC.
375 Park Avenue
New York, NY 10022
(212) 371-1110

Contact Person: Miss Lottie L. Jeffers, Secretary-Treasurer
Geographic Giving Pattern: Primarily local
Special Interest: Hospitals, welfare funds, church support
Religious Preference: Protestant, Roman Catholic, Jewish

CONSTANS-CULVER FOUNDATION
c/o Manufacturers Hanover Trust Company
600 Fifth Avenue
New York, NY 10020
(212) 957-1522

Contact Person: T.T. McKeever, Jr., Vice-President
Geographic Giving Pattern: Primarily local
Special Interest: Church support
Religious Preference: Protestant, Roman Catholic, Jewish

DULA (THE CALEB C. AND JULIA W.) EDUCATIONAL AND CHARITABLE FOUNDATION
c/o Manufacturers Hanover Trust Company
600 Fifth Avenue
New York, NY 10020
(212) 957-1222

Contact Person: Manufacturers Hanover Trust Co., Trustee
Geographic Giving Pattern: Primarily New York and St. Louis,
Missouri
Special Interest: Church support
Religious Preference: Greek Orthodox, Episcopalian

EBSARY CHARITABLE FOUNDATION, THE
920 Temple Building
Rochester, NY 14604
(716) 325-5307

Contact Person: Frank W. Allen, President
Geographic Giving Pattern: Primarily local
Special Interest: Protestant and Roman Catholic church support, higher education, welfare, youth agencies, cultural organizations

GOODMAN FAMILY FOUNDATION, THE
c/o Roy M. Goodman
1035 Fifth Avenue
New York, NY 10028
(212) 288-9067

Contact Person: Roy M. Goodman, President
Geographic Giving Pattern: Primarily local
Special Interest: Church and temple support, hospitals, and medical research
Religious Preference: Protestant, Roman Catholic, Jewish

HAGEDORN FUND, THE
c/o Manufacturers Hanover Trust Co.
600 Fifth Avenue
New York, NY 10020
(212) 975-1642

Contact Person: W.J. Fischer, Jr., Vice-President
Geographic Giving Pattern: Primarily New York
Special Interest: Theological seminaries, church support, religious associations
Religious Preference: Protestant, Roman Catholic

HEARST FOUNDATION, INC. THE
888 Seventh Avenue, 27th Floor
New York, NY 10106
(212) 586-5404

Contact Person: Robert M. Freshe, Jr., Executive Director for programs headquartered east of the Mississippi River
Geographic Giving Pattern: Within the United States and possessions
Special Interest: Poverty level and minority groups, education at all levels, health and medical research, cultural and religious programs
Religious Preference: Protestant, Roman Catholic, Jewish

KRESEVICH FOUNDATION, INC., THE
184 West 237 Street
Bronx, NY 10463

Contact Person: Felice Zambetti, President
Special Interest: Roman Catholic religious associations, church support. Some support for Jewish programs

LUCE (THE HENRY) FOUNDATION, INC.
111 W. 50th Street
New York, NY 10020
(212) 489-7700

Contact Person: Robert E. Armstrong, Executive Director
Geographic Giving Pattern: National, international
Special Interest: Theology
Religious Preference: Protestant, Roman Catholic, Jewish

MCCANN (JAMES J.) CHARITABLE TRUST
35 Market Street
Poughkeepsie, NY 12601
(914) 454-1110

Contact Person: John J. Gartland, Jr., Trustee
Geographic Giving Pattern: Primarily Dutchess County, New York
Special Interest: Education and research, arts, community service,
   health and medicine, church and religious associations
Religious Preference: Roman Catholic, Protestant

MICHEL (BARBARA AND CLIFFORD) FOUNDATION, INC.
80 Pine Street
New York, NY 10005
(212) 344-3091

Contact Person: James E. Alexander, Treasurer
Geographic Giving Pattern: Primarily local
Special Interest: Church support, education, hospitals
Religious Preference: Protestant, Roman Catholic

MONTEREY FUND, INC.
c/o Bear, Stearns & Company
5 Hanover Square
New York, NY 10004

Contact Person: Carl Holstrom, President
Geographic Giving Pattern: Primarily local
Special Interest: Educational institutions, welfare funds, hospitals,
   churches and synagogues
Religious Preference: Jewish, Roman Catholic, Protestant

ROCKEFELLER BROTHERS FUND
1290 Avenue of the Americas
New York, NY 10104
(212) 397-4800

Contact Person: Benjamin R. Shute, Jr., Secretary
Geographic Giving Pattern: National, international
Religious Preference: Protestant, Roman Catholic

101

ROCKEFELLER FOUNDATION, THE
1133 Avenue of the Americas
New York, NY 10036
(212) 869-8500

Contact Person: Laurence D. Stifel, Vice-President and Secretary
Geographic Giving Pattern: National, international
Religious Preference: Protestant, Roman Catholic, Jewish

North Carolina

BLUMENTHAL FOUNDATION, THE
P.O. Box 34689
Charlotte, NC 28234
(704) 377-6555

Contact Person: Herman Blumenthal, Chairman
Geographic Giving Pattern: Primarily in North Carolina
Special Interest: Conferences to promote understanding among
   religions. Also supports religious, educational, and welfare
   organizations
Religious Preference: Protestant, Roman Catholic, Jewish

RIXSON (OSCAR C.) FOUNDATION, INC.
535 Glendale Drive
Statesville, NC 28677
(704) 837-1550

Contact Person: Walter J. Munro, Jr., President
Special Interest: Needy active and retired religious workers. Also
   religious and charitable organizations
Religious Preference: Protestant, Roman Catholic

Ohio

ANDERSON FOUNDATION
P.O. Box 119
Maumee, OH 43537
(419) 893-5050

Contact Person: Kim Priest, Secretary to the Chairman
Geographic Giving Pattern: Primarily Toledo, Ohio
Special Interest: Education, religious organizations, churches,
   community funds
Religious Preference: Protestant, Roman Catholic, Jewish

VAN HUFFEL (THE I.J.) FOUNDATION
The Union Savings & Trust Company
106 Market Street
Warren, OH 44481
(216) 841-7882

Contact Person: The Union Savings & Trust Co., Trustee
Geographic Giving Pattern: National
Special Interest: Religious, educational, charitable
Religious Preference: Protestant, Roman Catholic

Oregon

COLLINS FOUNDATION
909 Terminal Sales Building
Portland, OR 97205
(503) 227-1219

Contact Person: William C. Pine, Executive Vice-President
Geographic Giving Pattern: Oregon
Special Interest: Education - higher and secondary, particularly
  science education, church support, youth and health agencies,
  social welfare
Religious Preference: Protestant, Roman Catholic

Pennsylvania

CONNELLY FOUNDATION
9300 Ashton Road
Philadelphia, PA 19136
(215) 698-5203

Contact Person: John F. Connelly, President
Geographic Giving Pattern: Primarily Philadelphia
Special Interest: Universities, colleges, schools, churches and
  hospitals
Religious Preference: Protestant, Roman Catholic, Jewish

Texas

FARISH (THE WILLIAM STAMPS) FUND
1100 Louisiana, Suite 4500
Houston, TX 77002
(713) 757-7313

Contact Person: W.S. Farish III, President
Geographic Giving Pattern: Primarily local
Special Interest: Theological seminaries, Episcopal church support
Religious Preference: Protestant, Roman Catholic

O'CONNOR (THE KATHRYN) FOUNDATION
400 Victoria Bank & Trust Building
Victoria, TX 77901

Contact Person: Dennis O'Connor, President
Geographic Giving Pattern: Primarily local
Special Interest: Advancement of religion, education and relief
of poverty
Religious Preference: Protestant, Roman Catholic

Virginia

WASHINGTON FORREST FOUNDATION
2300 Ninth Street, South
Arlington, VA 22204
(703) 920-2200

Contact Person: Berryman Davis, Executive Director
Geographic Giving Pattern: Northern Virginia
Special Interest: Religion, education, arts and humanities, health,
science, welfare
Religious Preference: Protestant, Roman Catholic

Wisconsin

CUDAHY (PATRICK AND ANNA M.) FUND
P.O. Box 11978
Milwaukee, WI 53211
(414) 765-0350

Contact Person: Richard W. Yeo, Administrator
Geographic Giving Pattern: Primarily local
Religious Preference: Protestant, Roman Catholic, Jewish

PRESTO FOUNDATION
3925 N. Hastings Way
Eau Claire, WI 54701

Contact Person: Melvin S. Cohen, Manager
Geographic Giving Pattern: National
Special Interest: Churches, schools, health and social agencies
Religious Preference: Protestant, Roman Catholic, Jewish

VILTER FOUNDATION, INC.
2217 South First Street
Milwaukee, WI 53207
(414) 744-0111

Contact Person: A.A. Silverman, President
Geographic Giving Pattern: Primarily local
Special Interest: Churches, education - higher and secondary,
religious welfare funds
Religious Preference: Protestant, Roman Catholic, Jewish

Other Foundations

Alabama

MALBIS MEMORIAL FOUNDATION
c/o Antigone Papageorge
P.O. Box 218
Daphne, AL 36526
(205) 626-3050
Contact Person: C.D. Papadeas, President
Geographic Giving Pattern: Local
Special Interest: Primarily religious; Greek Orthodox

California

PEERY (RICHARD T.) FOUNDATION
2560 Mission College Blvd., Suite 101
Santa Clara, CA 95000
(408) 980-0130
Contact Person: Richard T. Peery
Geographic Giving Pattern: International
Special Interest: Mormon Church

PHILIBOSIAN (STEPHEN) FOUNDATION
21506 West Pacific Coast Highway
Malibu, CA 90265
(213) 456-2937
Contact Person: Joyce Stein, Trustee
Geographic Giving Pattern: International
Special Interest: Missionary, educational and social programs for the
    Armenian-American church including aid for Armenian schools
    in the Middle East

Kansas

SCHOWALTER FOUNDATION, INC., THE
716 Main Street
Newton, KS 67114
(316) 283-3720
Contact Person: William L. Friesen, President
Geographic Giving Pattern: Primarily Midwest, some international
Special Interest: Retired ministers and missionaries, theological
    seminaries and church-related schools
Religious Preference: Mennonite

Louisiana

HELIS FOUNDATION, THE
912 Whitney Building
New Orleans, LA 70130
(504) 523-1831

Contact Person: A.E. Armbruster, Vice-President
Geographic Giving Pattern: Primarily local
Special Interest: Support for church and religious organizations, higher education
Religious Preference: Greek Orthodox

Massachusetts

DEMOULAS FOUNDATION
875 East Street
Tewksbury, MA 01876
(617) 851-7381

Contact Person: Telemachus A. Demoulas
Geographic Giving Pattern: Primarily local
Special Interest: Greek Orthodox church support, higher and secondary education

Michigan

MANOOGIAN (ALEX AND MARIA) FOUNDATION
3001 W. Big Beaver, Suite 520
Troy, MI 48084

Contact Person: Alex Manoogian, President
Geographic Giving Pattern: General
Special Interest: Armenian welfare funds, religious organizations, churches, education and cultural programs

MARDIGIAN FOUNDATION
1525 Tottenham
Birmingham, MI 48009
(313) 589-3804

Contact Person: Edward Mardigian, Sr., President
Geographic Giving Pattern: National
Special Interest: Armenian church and cultural support, religious associations and welfare funds

Appendix A

The Foundation Center has a nationwide network of reference collections for free public use which fall within four basic categories. The reference libraries operated by the Center offer the widest variety of user services and the most comprehensive collections of foundation materials, including all Center publications; books, services and periodicals on philanthropy; and foundation annual reports, newsletters and press clippings. The New York and Washington, D.C. libraries contain the IRS returns for all currently active private foundations in the U.S. The Cleveland and San Francisco field offices contain IRS records for those foundations in the midwestern and western states, respectively.

Cooperating collections contain IRS records for those foundations within their own state, and a complete collection of Foundation Center publications. Local affiliate collections (*) provide a core collection of Center publications for free public use.

Some reference collections (•) are operated by foundations or area associations of foundations. They are often able to offer special materials or provide extra services, such as seminars or orientations for users, because of their close relationship to the local philanthropic community. All other collections are operated by cooperating libraries or other nonprofit agencies. Many are located within public institutions and all are open to the public during a regular schedule of hours.

Please telephone individual libraries for more information about their holdings or hours. To check on new locations call toll-free 800-424-9836 for current information.

Where to Go for Information on Foundation Funding

REFERENCE COLLECTIONS OPERATED BY THE FOUNDATION CENTER

The Foundation Center
888 Seventh Avenue
NEW YORK, New York 10106
212-975-1120

The Foundation Center
1001 Connecticut Avenue, NW
WASHINGTON, D.C. 20036
202-331-1400

The Foundation Center
Kent H. Smith Library
739 National City Bank Bldg.
629 Euclid
CLEVELAND, Ohio 44114
216-861-1933

The Foundation Center
312 Sutter Street
SAN FRANCISCO, Calif. 94108
415-397-0902

COOPERATING COLLECTIONS

Alabama

Birmingham Public Library
2020 Park Place
Birmingham 35203
205-254-2541

Auburn University at
   Montgomery Library
Montgomery 36193
205-279-9110

Alaska

University of Alaska, Anchorage Library
3211 Providence Drive
Anchorage 99504
907-263-1848

Arizona

Phoenix Public Library
Social Scientist Subject Department
12 East McDowell Road
Phoenix 85004
602-262-4782

Tucson Public Library
Main Library
200 South Sixth Avenue
Tucson 85701
602-791-4393

Arkansas

Westark Community College Library
Grand Avenue at Waldron Rd.
Fort Smith 72913
501-785-4241

Little Rock Public Library
Reference Department
700 Louisiana Street
Little Rock 72201
501-370-5950

California

California Community Foundation •
Funding Information Center
1151 West Sixth Street
Los Angeles 90017
213-413-4719

Riverside Public Library *
3581 7th Street
Riverside 92501
714-787-7201

California State Library *
Reference Services, Rm. 309
914 Capitol Mall
Sacramento 95814
916-322-0369

San Diego Public Library
820 E Street
San Diego 92101
619-236-5565

Orange County Community
  Development Council *
1440 East First Street, 4th floor
Santa Ana 92701
714-547-6801

Santa Barbara Public Library
Reference Section
40 East Anapamu
P.O. Box 1019
Santa Barbara 93102
805-962-7653

Central Sierra Arts Council *
19411 Village Drive
Sonora 95370
209-532-2787

North Coast Opportunities, Inc. *
101 West Church Street
Ukiah 95482
707-462-1954

Colorado

Pikes Peak Library District *
20 North Cascade Avenue
Colorado Springs 80901
303-473-2080

Denver Public Library
Sociology Division
1357 Broadway
Denver 80203
303-571-2190

Connecticut

Hartford Public Library
Reference Department
500 Main Street
Hartford 06103
203-525-9121

D.A.T.A.*
81 Saltonstall Avenue
New Haven 06513
203-776-0797

Delaware

Hugh Morris Library
University of Delaware
Newark 19711
302-738-2965

Florida

Jacksonville Public Library
Business, Science, and Industry
Department
122 North Ocean Street
Jacksonville 32202
904-633-3926

Miami-Dade Public Library
Florida Collection
One Biscayne Boulevard
Miami 33132
305-579-5001

Orlando Public Library *
10 North Rosalind
Orlando 32801
305-425-4694

Leon County Public Library *
Community Funding Resources Center
1940 North Monroe Street
Tallahassee 32303
904-487-2665

Selby Public Library *
1001 Boulevard of the Arts
Sarasota 33577
813-366-7303

Georgia

Atlanta Public Library
1 Margaret Mitchell Square at Forsyth
    and Carnegie Way
Atlanta 30303
404-688-4636

Hawaii

Thomas Hale Hamilton Library
General Reference
University of Hawaii
2550 The Mall
Honolulu 96822
808-948-7214

Community Research Center * •
The Hawaiian Foundation
Financial Plaza of the Pacific
111 South King Street
Honolulu 96813
808-525-8548

Idaho

Caldwell Public Library
1010 Dearborn Street
Caldwell 83605
208-459-3242

Illinois

Belleville Public Library *
121 E. Washington Street
Belleville 62220
618-234-0441

Donors Forum of Chicago •
208 South LaSalle Street
Chicago 60604
312-726-4882

DuPage Township *
300 Briarcliff Road
Bolingbrook 60439
312-759-1317

Sangamon State University Library
Shepherd Road
Springfield 62708
217-786-6633

Indiana

Allen County Public Library *
900 Webster Street
Fort Wayne 46802
219-424-7241

Indiana University Nortwest Library *
3400 Broadway
Gary 46408
219-980-6580

Indianapolis-Marion County
   Public Library
40 East St. Clair Street
Indianapolis 46204
317-269-1733

Iowa

Public Library of Des Moines
100 Locust Street
Des Moines 50308
515-283-4259

Kansas

Topeka Public Library
Adult Services Department
1515 West Tenth Street
Topeka 66604
913-233-2040

Wichita Public Libaray *
223 South Main
Wichita 67202
316-262-0611

Kentucky

The Louisville Foundation, Inc. * •
623 West Main Street
Louisville 40202
502-585-4649

Louisville Free Public Library
Fourth and York Streets
Louisville 40203
502-584-4154

Louisiana

East Baton Rouge Parish Library
Centroplex Library
120 St. Louis Street
Baton Rouge 70802
504-344-5291

New Orleans Public Library
Business and Science Division
219 Loyola Avenue
New Orleans 70140
504-524-7382, ext. 33

Shreve Memorial Library *
424 Texas Street
Shreveport 71101
318-226-5894

Maine

University of Southern Maine
Center for Research and Advanced
  Study
246 Deering Avenue
Portland 04102
207-780-4411

Maryland

Enoch Pratt Free Library
Social Science and History Department
400 Cathedral Street
Baltimore 21201
301-396-5320

Massachusetts

Associated Grantmakers of Massachusetts *
294 Washington Street
Suite 501
Boston 02108
617-426-2608

Boston Public Library
Copley Square
Boston 02117
617-536-5400

Walpole Public Library *
Walcott Avenue at Union Street
East Walpole 02032
617-668-0232

Western Massachusetts Funding Resource
  Center *
Campaign for Human Development
Chancery Annex
73 Chestnut Street
Springfield 01103
413-732-3175, ext. 67

Grants Resource Center *
Worcester Public Libray
Salem Square
Worcester 01608
617-799-1655

Michigan

Alpena County Library
211 North First Avenue
Alpena 49707
517-356-6188

Henry Ford Centennial Library
16301 Michigan Avenue
Dearborn 48126
313-943-2337

Purdy Library
Wayne State University
Detroit 48202
313-577-4040

Michigan State University Libraries
Reference Library
East Lansing 48824
517-353-8816

Farmington Community Library *
32737 West 12 Mile Road
Farmington Hills 48018
313-553-0300

University of Michigan-Flint Library
Reference Department
Flint 48503
313-762-3408

Grand Rapids Public Library
Sociology and Education Dept.
Library Plaza
Grand Rapids 49503
616-456-4411

Michigan Technological University
  Library
Highway U.S. 41
Houghton 49931
906-487-2507

Minnesota

Duluth Public Library *
520 Superior Street
Duluth 55802
218-723-3802

Minneapolis Public Library
Sociology Department
300 Nicollet Mall
Minneapolis 55401
612-372-6555

Saint Paul Public Library *
90 West Fourth Street
Saint Paul 55102
612-292-6311

Mississippi

Jackson Metropolitan Library
301 North State Street
Jackson 39201
601-944-1120

Missouri

Clearinghouse for Mid-continent
    Foundations
Univ. of Missouri, Kansas City
Law School, Suite 1-300
52nd Street and Oak
Kansas City 64113
816-276-1176

Kansas City Public Library
311 East 12th Street
Kansas City 64106
816-221-2685

Metropolitan Association for
    Philanthropy, Inc. *
5600 Oakland, G-324
St. Louis 63110
314-647-2290

Springfield-Greene County Library
397 East Central Street
Springfield 65801
417-866-4636

Montana

Eastern Montana College Library
Reference Department
Billings 59101
406-657-2262

Montana State Library *
Reference Department
1515 E. 6th Avenue
Helena 59620
406-449-3004

Nebraska

W. Dale Clark Library
Social Sciences Department
215 South 15th Steet
Omaha 68102
402-444-4822

Nevada

Clark County Library
1401 East Flamingo Road
Las Vegas 89109
702-733-7810

Washoe County Library
301 South Center Street
Reno 89505
702-785-4190

New Hampshire

The New Hampshire Charitable Fund •
One South Street
Concord 03301
603-225-6641

Littleton Public Library *
109 Main Street
Littleton 03561
603-444-5741

New Jersey

The Support Center *
17 Academy St., Suite 1101
Newark 07102
201-643-5774

New Jersey State Library
Government Reference Unit
185 West State Street
P.O. Box 1898
Trenton 08625
609-292-6220

New Mexico

Albuquerque Community Foundation * •
6400 Uptown Boulevard, N.E.
Suite 500-W
Albuquerque 87110
505-883-6240

New Mexico State Library
325 Don Gaspar Street
Santa Fe 87503
505-827-3824

New York

New York State Library
Cultural Education Center
Humanities Section
Empire State Plaza
Albany 12230
518-474-7645

Buffalo and Erie County Public Library
Lafayette Square
Buffalo 14203
716-856-7525

Levittown Public Library
Reference Department
One Bluegrass Lane
Levittown 11756
516-731-5728

Plattsburgh Public Library
Reference Department
15 Oak Street
Plattsburgh 12901
518-563-0921

Rochester Public Library
Business and Social Sciences Division
115 South Avenue
Rochester 14604
716-428-7328

Onondaga County Pubic Library
335 Montgomery Street
Syracuse 13202
315-473-4491

White Plains Public Library *
100 Martine Avenue
White Plains 10601
914-682-4488

North Carolina

North Carolina State Library
109 East Jones Street
Raleigh 27611
919-733-3270

The Winston-Salem Foundation •
229 First Union National Bank Bldg.
Winston-Salem 27101
919-725-2382

North Dakota

Western Dakota Grants Resource Center *
Bismarck Junior College Library
Bismarck 58501
701-224-5450

The Library, North Dakota State
    University
Fargo 58105
701-237-8876

Ohio

Public Library of Cincinnati and
    Hamilton County
Education Department
800 Vine Street
Cincinnati 45202
513-369-6940

Ohio Dept. of Economic and
  Community Development *
Office of Grants Assistance
30 E. Broad Street, 24th floor
Columbus 43215
614-466-6652

Toledo-Lucas County Public Library
Social Science Department
325 Michigan Street
Toledo 43624
419-255-7055, ext. 221

Oklahoma

Oklahoma City University Library
NW 23rd at North Blackwelder
Oklahoma City 73106
405-521-5072

Tulsa City-County Library System
400 Civic Center
Tulsa 74103
918-592-7944

Oregon

Library Association of Portland
Education and Documents
801 S.W. Tenth Avenue
Portland 97205
503-223-7201

Pennsylvania

Northhampton County Area
  Community College *
Learning Resources Center
3835 Green Pond Road
Bethlehem 18017
215-865-5358

Erie County Public Library *
3 South Perry Square
Erie 16501
814-452-2333, ext. 54

Dauphin County Library System *
Central Library
101 Walnut Street
Harrisburg 17101
717-234-4961

Lancaster Public Library *
125 North Duke Street
Lancaster 17602
717-394-2651

The Free Library of Philadelphia
Logan Square
Philadelphia 19103
215-686-5423

Hillman Library
University of Pittsburgh
Pittsburgh 15260
412-624-4528

Rhode Island

Providence Public Library
Reference Department
150 Empire Street
Providence 02903
401-521-7722

South Carolina

Charleston County Public Library *
404 King Street
Charleston 29403
803-723-1645

South Carolina State Library
Reader Services Department
1500 Senate Street
Columbia 29211
803-758-3181

South Dakota

South Dakota State Library
State Library Building
322 South Fort Street
Pierre 57501
605-773-3131

Tennessee

Knoxville-Knox County Public Library
500 West Church Avenue
Knoxville 37902
615-523-0781

Memphis Public Library
1850 Peabody Avenue
Memphis 38104
901-528-2957

Public Library of Nashville and Davidson
    County *
8th Avenue, North and Union Street
Nashville 37203
615-244-4700

Texas

The Hogg Foundation for Mental Health •
The University of Texas
Austin 78712
512-471-5041

Corpus Christi State University Library
6300 Ocean Drive
Corpus Christi 78412
512-991-6810

Dallas Public Library
Grants Information Service
1515 Young Street
Dallas 75201
214-749-4100

El Paso Community Foundation •
El Paso National Bank Bldg., Suite 1616
El Paso 79901
915-533-4020

Funding Information Center *
Texas Christian University Library
Ft. Worth 76129
817-921-7000, ext. 6130

Houston Public Library
Bibliography & Information Center
500 McKinney Avenue
Houston 77002
713-224-5441, ext. 265

Funding Information Library
1120 Milam Building
115 E. Travis Street
San Antonio 78205
512-227-4333

Utah

Salt Lake City Public Library
Business and Science Department
209 East Fifth South
Salt Lake City 84111
801-363-5733

Vermont

State of Vermont Department of
    Libraries
References Services Unit
111 State Street
Montpellier 05602
802-828-3261

Virginia

Grants Resources Library
Ninth Floor
Hampton City Hall
Hampton 23669
804-272-6496

Richmond Public Library
Business, Science, & Technology Dept.
101 East Franklin Street
Richmond 23219
804-780-8223

Washington

Seattle Public Library
1000 Fourth Avenue
Seattle 98104
206-625-4881

Spokane Public Library
Funding Information Center
West 906 Main Avenue
Spokane 99201
509-838-3361

West Virginia

Kanawha County Public Library
123 Capitol Street
Charleston 25301
304-343-4646

Wisconsin

Marquette University Memorial Library
1415 West Wisconsin Avenue
Milwaukee 53233
414-224-1515

Wyoming

Laramie County Community College
  Library
1400 East College Drive
Cheyenne 82001
307-634-5853

Canada

Canadian Centre for Philanthropy •
185 Bay Street, Suite 504
Toronto, Ontario M5J 1K6
416-364-4875

England

Charities Aid Foundation *
12 Crane Court
Fleet Street
London EC4A 2JJ
1-583-7772

Mexico

Biblioteca Benjamin Franklin
Londres 16
Mexico City 6, D.F.
525-591-0244

Puerto Rico

Universidad del Sagrado Corazon
M.M.T. Guevarra Library
Correo Galle Loiza
Santurce 00914
809-728-1515, ext. 343

Virgin Islands

College of the Virgin Islands Library
Saint Thomas
U.S. Virgin Islands 00801
809-774-9200, ext. 487

Appendix B

DIRECTORIES OF
STATE AND LOCAL GRANTMAKERS

A Bibliography Compiled by Lydia T. Motyka, Librarian

Alabama (184 foundations). *Alabama Foundation Directory*. Edited by Anne F. Knight. 1980. 25 p. Based primarily on 1978 990-PF and 990-AR returns filed with the IRS. Main section arranged alphabetically by foundation; entries include areas of interest and officers; no sample grants. Indexes of geographic areas and major areas of interest. Available from Reference Department, Birmingham Public Library, 2020 Park Place, Birmingham, Alabama 35203. $ 5.00 prepaid.

California (approximately 500 foundations). *Guide to California Foundations*. 4th edition. Prepared by Melinda Marble. 1981. xix, 409 p. Based primarily on 1979 990-PF and 990-AR returns filed with the IRS or records in the California Attorney General's Office; some additional data supplied by foundations completing questionnaires. Main section arranged alphabetically by foundation; entries include statement of purpose, sample grants, and officers. Also sections on applying for grants, scholarship foundations, and a glossary of terms. Indexes of all foundations by name and by county location; index of primary interests only for those foundations completing questionnaire. Available from *Guide to California Foundations*, 210 Post Street, #814, San Francisco, California 94108. Make check or money order payable to Northern California Grantmakers. $9.00 prepaid.

California (620 corporations). *National Directory of Corporate Charity: California Edition*. Compiled by Sam Sternberg. 1981. x, 450+ p. Based on annual reports, questionnaires, reference directories, grants lists, corporate donors lists of non-profit organizations, and news releases. Main section arranged alphabetically by corporation; entries include categories of giving, giving policies, geographic preference, and contact person; no sample grants. Also sections describing corporate giving patterns, non-profit strategy and corporate giving, how to conduct a corporate solicitation campaign, and a bibliography. Indexes of operating locations of corporations, support categories, and companies and their California subsidiaries. Available from Regional Young Adult Project, 330 Ellis Street, Room 506, San Francisco, California 94102.

California (73 foundations). *San Diego County Foundation Directory 1980.* Compiled by The Community Congress of San Diego, Inc. 1980. 72 p. Based on 1977 through 1979 CT-2 forms filed with the California Attorney General's Office. Main section arranged alphabetically by foundation; entries include statement of purpose and contact person; no sample grants. Index of foundation names. Appendixes of San Diego County foundation grants and officers and trustees. Available from Congress of San Diego, 1172 Morena Boulevard, San Diego, California 92110. $10.00 prepaid.

California (45 Bay Area foundations). *Small Change from Big Bucks: A Report and Recommendations on Bay Area Foundations and Social Change.* Edited by Herb Allen and Sam Sternberg. 1979. 226 p. Based primarily on 1976 990-AR returns filed with the IRS, CT-2 forms filed with California, annual reports, and interviews with foundations. Main section arranged alphabetically by foundation; entries include statement of purpose and contact person; no sample grants. Also sections on the Bay Area Community for Responsive Philanthropy, foundations and social change, the study methodology, the committee's findings, and the committee's recommendations. No indexes. Appendixes of Bay Area resources for technical assistance, bibliography, nonprofit organizations in law and fact, and glossary. Available from Regional Young Adult Project, 330 Ellis Street, Room 506, San Francisco, California 94102. Make check payable to: Regional Young Adult Project. $3.00 plus $1.50 postage.

California (525 foundations). *Where the Money's At, How to Reach Over 500 California Grant-Making Foundations.* Edited by Patricia Blair Tobey with Irving R. Warner as contributing editor. 1978. 536 p. Based on 1975 through 1977 (mainly 1976) California CT-2 forms in the California Registry of Charitable Trusts Office. Main section arranged alphabetically by foundation; entries include statement of purpose, sample grants, and officers. Indexes of foundation names, foundation names within either Northern or Southern California, counties, and foundation personnel. Available from Irving R. Warner, 3235 Berry Drive, Studio City, California 91604. $17.00.

Colorado (approximately 192 foundations). *Colorado Foundation Directory 1981-82.* 3rd edition. Co-sponsored by the Junior League of Denver, Inc., the Denver Foundation, and the Attorney General of Colorado. 1982. 106 p. Based on 1979 through 1981 (mostly 1980) 990-PF and 990-AR returns filed with the IRS and information supplied by foundations. Main section arranged alphabetically by foundation; entries include statement of purpose, sample grants, and officers. Also sections on proposal writing, sample proposal, and sample budget form. Available from Colorado Foundation Directory, Junior League of Denver, Inc.,

1805 South Bellaire, Suite 400, Denver, Colorado 80222. Make check payable to: Colorado Foundation Directory. $10.00 prepaid.

Connecticut (61 foundations). *Directory of the Major Connecticut Foundations.* Compiled by Logos, Inc. 1982. 49 p. Based on 1979-80 990-PF and 990-AR IRS returns, foundation publications and information from the Office of the Attorney General in Hartford. Arranged alphabetically by foundation; entries include grant range, sample grants, geographic limitations, officers and directors. Index of subjects. Available from Logos, Inc., 7 Park Street, Room 212, Attleboro, Massachusetts 02703. $19.95 prepaid.

Connecticut (approximately 465 foundations). *1981 Connecticut Foundation Directory.* Edited by Michael E. Burns. 1982. 148 p. Based primarily on 1980 and 1981 990-PF and 990-AR returns filed with the IRS. Main section arranged alphabetically by foundation; entries include complete grants list and principal officer. No statement of purpose or indexes. Available from OUA/DATA, 81 Saltonstall Avenue, New Haven, Connecticut 06513. $15.00 prepaid.

Connecticut (approximately 769 corporations). *1983 Guide to Corporate Giving in Connecticut.* Edited by Michael E. Burns and compiled by Anne Washburn. 1982. 374 p. Based on information supplied by corporations. Main section arranged alphabetically by corporation; entries for most corporations include areas of interest, giving policies, geographic preference, and contact person; some sample grants. Indexes of corporations, by town. Available from OUA/DATA, 81 Saltonstall Avenue, New Haven, Connecticut 06513. $20.00 plus $1.50 postage.

Delaware (558 foundations). *Delaware Foundations.* Compiled by United Way of Delaware, Inc. 1979. viii, 116 p. Based on 1976 through 1978 990-PF and 990-AR returns filed with the IRS, annual reports, and information supplied by foundations. Main section arranged alphabetically by foundation; entries include statement of purpose and officers; no sample grants. Detailed information on 96 private foundations, a sampling of company-sponsored foundations and corporate giving programs and lists of 24 operating foundations and 438 out-of-state foundations. No indexes. Available from United Way of Delaware, Inc., 701 Shipley Street, Wilmington, Delaware 19801. $7.50 prepaid.

District of Columbia (approximately 500 foundations). *The Washington D.C. Metropolitan Area Foundation Directory.* Edited by Julia Mills Jacobsen and Kay Carter Courtade. 1979. 80 p. Based on 1976 and 1977 990-PF and 990-AR returns filed with the IRS and information supplied by foundations. Main section arranged alphabetically by foundation; entries include statement of purpose, sample grants, and officers. Also sections listing nongrantmaking foundations, operating foundations, inactive foundations, and dissolved foundations. Indexes of foundation names and officers and trustees. Available from Management Communications, Publications Division, 4416 Edmunds Street, N.W., Washington, D.C. 20007. $13.50.

Georgia (approximately 550 foundations). *Georgia Foundation Directory.* Compiled by Ann Bush. 1979. 28 p. Based on 1976 through 1978 990-PF and 990-AR returns filed with the IRS. Contains three sections: I. Alphabetical listing by foundation name, II. City listing by foundation name, III. Subject listing by foundation name. Entries do not include foundation address, purpose statement, sample grants, or officers. No indexes. Available from Foundation Collection, Atlanta Public Library, 10 Pryor Street, S.W., Atlanta, Georgia 30303. Free.

Georgia (530 foundations). *Guide to Foundations in Georgia.* Compiled by the Georgia Department of Human Resources. 1978. xv, 145 p. Based on 1975 through 1977 990-PF and 990-AR returns filed with the IRS. Main section arranged alphabetically by foundation; entries include statement of purpose, sample grants, and principal officer. Indexes of foundation names, cities, and program interests. Available from State Economic Opportunity Unit, Office of District Programs, Department of Human Resources, 618 Ponce de Leon Avenue, N.E., Atlanta, Georgia 30308. Free. September 1981 Addendum available from same address. Free.

Hawaii (55 foundations and 6 church funding sources). *A Guide to Charitable Trusts and Foundations in the State of Hawaii.* 1981. 62 + p. Based on 990-PF and 990-AR returns filed in the State Attorney General's Office, annual reports, and information supplied by foundations. Main section arranged alphabetically by foundation; entries include statement of purpose, sample grants for some foundations, and officers. No indexes. Available from Director of Planning and Development, Alu Like, Inc., 2828 Paa Street, Honolulu, Hawaii 96819. $15.00 for nonprofit organizations, $25.00 for profit-making organizations.

Idaho (78 foundations). *Directory of Idaho Foundations.* 2nd edition. Prepared by the Caldwell Public Library. 1980. 12 p.Based on mostly 1978 and 1979 990-PF and 990-AR returns filed with the IRS. Main section arranged alphabetically by foundation; entries include areas of interest. No sample grants, officers, or indexes. Available from the Foundation Collection, Caldwell Public Library, 1010 Dearborn Street, Caldwell, Idaho 83605. $1.00 prepaid and $.28 in postage stamps.

Illinois (approximately 175 corporations). *The Chicago Corporate Connection: A Directory of Chicago Area Corporate Contributors, Including Downstate Illinois and Northern Indiana.* Edited by Susan M. Levy. 1981. xii, 109 p. Based on information supplied by corporations. Main section arranged alphabetically by corporation; entries include principal business activity, giving policies, geographic preference, and contact person; no areas of interest or sample grants. Also section on guidelines for seeking corporate funding and a bibliography. Indexes of geographic locations and fields of business. Available from Donors Forum of Chicago, 208 South LaSalle, Chicago, Illinois 60604. $8.50 prepaid.

Illinois (approximately 1900 foundations). *Illinois Foundation Directory.* Edited by Beatrice J. Capriotti and Frank J. Capriotti III. 1978. ix, 527 + p. Based on mostly 1976 and 1977 990-PF and 990-AR returns filed with the IRS plus correspondence with some foundations. Main section arranged alphabetically by foundation; entries include statement of purpose, sample grants, and officers. Table of contents alphabetical by foundation name; no indexes. Available from the Foundation Data Center, Kenmar Center, 401 Kenmar Circle, Minnetonka, Minnesota 55343. $425 (includes seminar). Update service by annual subscription. $200.

Indiana (265 foundations). *Indiana Foundations: A Directory.* Edited by Paula Reading Spear. 1979. iii, 175 p. Based on 1977 through 1979 (mostly 1978) 990-PF and 990-AR returns filed with the IRS and information supplied by foundations. Main section arranged alphabetically by foundation; entries include areas of interest, sample grants, and contact person. Indexes of financial criteria, subjects, and counties. Appendixes of restricted foundations, foundations for student assistance only, and dissolved foundations. Available from Central Research Systems, 320 North Meridian, Suite 1011, Indianapolis, Indiana 46204. $19.95 prepaid.

Kansas (approximately 255 foundations). *Directory of Kansas Foundations.* Edited by Connie Townsley. 1979. 128 p. Based on 990-PF and 990-AR returns filed with the IRS. Fiscal date of information not provided. Main section arranged alphabetically by foundation; entries include areas of interest, sample grants, and officers. Index of cities. Available from Association of Community Arts Councils of Kansas, Columbian Building, 4th Floor, 112 West 6th, Topeka, Kansas 66603. $5.80 prepaid.

Kentucky (117 foundations). *Foundation Profiles of the Southeast: Kentucky, Tennessee, Virginia.* Edited by James H. Taylor, and John L. Wilson, 1981. vi, 153 p. Based on 1978 and 1979 990-PF and 990-AR IRS returns. Main section arranged alphabetically by foundation; entries include assets, total number and amount of grants, sample grants and officers. No indexes. Available from James H. Taylor Associates, Inc., 804 Main Street, Williamsburg, Kentucky 40769. $39.95 prepaid.

Kentucky (101 foundations). *A Guide to Kentucky Grantmakers.* Edited by Nancy. C. Dougherty. 1982. 19 p. Based on questionnaires to foundations, 1981 990-PF and 990-AR IRS returns. Arranged alphabetically by foundation; entries include assets, total grants paid, number of grants, smallest/largest grant, primary area of interest and contact person. No indexes. Available from The Louisville Foundation, Inc., 623 West Main Street, Louisville, Kentucky 40202. $7.50 prepaid.

Maine (139 foundations). *A Directory of Foundations in the State of Maine.* 3rd edition. Compiled by the Center for Research and Advanced Study. 1980. ii, 59 p. Based on 1979 and 1980 990-PF and 990-AR returns filed with the IRS. Main section arranged alphabetically by city location of foundation; entries include areas of interest, sample grants, and principal officer. Also sections on basic elements in a letter of inquiry, a bibliography, a description of IRS information returns, a sample report to funding source, and a list of recent grants. Index of subjects. Available from Center for Research and Advanced Study, University of Southern Maine, 246 Deering Avenue, Portland, Maine 04102. $3.00 prepaid.

Maine (59 corporations). *Maine Corporate Funding Directory.* 1981. xii, 56 p. Based on information supplied by corporations. Main section arranged alphabetically by corporation; entries include contact person and, for a few corporations, the areas of interest, geographic limitations, and sample grants. Indexes of corporations and areas of interest. Available from Center for Research and Advanced Study, University of Southern Maine, 246 Deering Avenue, Portland, Maine 04102. $5.50 prepaid.

Maryland (approximately 380 foundations). *1980 Annual Index Foundation Reports.* Compiled by the Office of the Attorney General. 1981. 203 p. Based on 1980 990-PF and 990-AR returns received by the Maryland State Attorney General's Office. Main section arranged alphabetically by foundation; entries include statement of purpose and sample grants for some foundations, complete list of grants, and officers. No indexes. Available from the Office of the Attorney General, One South Calvert Street, Baltimore, Maryland 21202. Attention: Sharon Smith. $35.00 prepaid.

Massachusetts (726 foundations). *Directory of Foundations in Massachusetts.* 1983. Based on 990-PF and 990-AR returns filed with the IRS. Prepared by office of the Attorney General of the Commonwealth of Massachusetts and the Associated Foundations of Greater Boston. Main section arranged in two parts—foundations which make grants primarily to organizations, and foundations which make grants primarily to individuals; entries include statement of purpose and officers; no sample grants. Appendixes of grant amounts, geographic restrictions, purposes, loans, non-scholarship loans, scholarships-restricted by city, scholarships-population groups, and scholarships-purpose restricted. Available from Associated Grantmakers of Massachusetts, 294 Washington Street, Suite 501, Boston, Massachusetts 02108.

Massachusetts (960 foundations). *A Directory of Foundations in the Commonwealth of Massachusetts.* Edited by John Parker Huber. 2nd edition. 1976.

xii, 161 p. Based on 1974 990-PF and 990-AR returns filed with the IRS. Main section arranged alphabetically by foundation; entries include sample grants and officers; no statement of purpose. Indexes of geographical areas and largest single grants awarded. Appendixes of additions including initial returns, relocations in Massachusetts, and previously existing foundations appearing for the first time and of deletions including final returns, relocations outside of Massachusetts, and first edition foundations not included because of lack of data. Available from Eastern Connecticut State College Foundation, Inc., P.O. Box 431, Willimantic, Connecticut 06226. $15.00 prepaid.

Massachusetts (56 Boston area foundaitons). *Directory of the Major Greater Boston Foundations.* 1981. 48 p. Based on 1975 through 1980 990-PF and 990-AR returns filed with the IRS. Main section arranged alphabetically by foundation; entries include statement of purpose, sample grants, and officers. Index of fields of interest. Available from Logos Associates, 12 Gustin, Attleboro, Massachusetts 02703. $19.95 prepaid.

Michigan (863 foundations). The Michigan Foundation Directory. 3rd edition. Prepared by the Council of Michigan Foundations and Michigan League for Human Services. 1980. vii, 113 p. Based on information compiled from foundations, the Foundation Center, and primarily 1978 tax returns filed with the IRS. Main section arranged in three parts: Section I is mainly an alphabetical listing of 304 Michigan foundations having assets of $200,000 or making annual grants of at least $25,000 with entries including statement of purpose and officers, but no sample grants; Section I also provides brief information on 774 foundations making grants of $1,000 or more annually, geographical listing of foundations by city, terminated foundations, and special purpose foundations; Section II is a survey of Michigan foundation philanthropy; and Section III provides information for seeking grants. Indexes of subject/areas of interest; donors, trustees, officers; and foundation names. Available from Michigan League for Human Services, 200 Mill Street, Lansing, Michigan 48933. $9.00 prepaid.

Minnesota (450 foundations). *Guide to Minnesota Foundations.* 2nd edition. Prepared by the Minnesota Council on Foundations. 1980. vii, 95 p. Based on mostly 1978 and 1979 990-PF and 990-AR returns filed with the IRS and date from cooperating foundations. Main section arranged alphabetically by foundation; entries for foundations with grant totals of $25,000 or more per year include statement of purpose, sample grants and officers. Also sections on smaller foundations, proposal writing, and the foundation review process. Index of foundation names. Available from Minnesota Council on Foundations, 413 Foshay Tower, Minneapolis, Minnesota 55402. $10.00 plus $.40 sales tax or your sales tax exempt number.

Minnesota (598 foundations). *Minnesota Foundation Directory*. Edited by Beatrice J. Capriotti and Frank J. Capriotti III. 1976. 274+ p. Based on 1973 and 1974 990-PF and 990-AR returns filed with the IRS. Main section arranged alphabetically by foundation; entries include statement of purpose, sample grants, and officers. Indexes of donors, administrators and trustees, and banks and trust companies as corporate trustees. Available from Foundation Data Center, Ridgedale State Bank Building, 1730 South Plymouth Road, Suite 202, Minnetonka, Minnesota 55343. $275. (Includes seminar and research training seminar.) Update service by annual subscription. $180.

Montana (42 Montana and 12 Wyoming foundations). *The Montana and Wyoming Foundations Directory*. Compiled by Paula Deigert, Jane Kavanaugh, and Ellen Alweis. 1981. 16 p. Based on 990-PF and 990-AR returns filed with the IRS, the *National Data Book*, and information supplied by foundations. Main section arranged alphabetically by foundation; entries include areas of interest and contact person; no sample grants. Indexes of foundation names and areas of interest. Available from Eastern Montana College Foundation, 1500 North 30th Street, Billings, Montana 59101. $5.00 prepaid.

Nebraska (approximately 154 foundations). *Nebraska Foundation Directory*. Compiled by the Junior League of Omaha. 1981. 14 p. Based on mostly 1979 and 1980 990-PF and 990-AR returns filed with the IRS. Main section arranged alphabetically by foundation; entries include statement of purpose and officers. No sample grants or indexes. Available from Junior League of Omaha, 808 South 74th Plaza, Omaha, Nebraska 68114. $3.00.

New Hampshire (approximately 400 foundations). *Directory of Charitable Funds in New Hampshire*. 3rd edition. June 1976. 107 p. Based on 1974 and 1975 records in the New Hampshire Attorney General's Office. Main section arranged alphabetically by foundation; entries include statement of purpose and officers; no sample grants. Indexes of geographical areas when restricted, and of purposes when not geographically restricted. Available from the Office of the Attorney General, Charitable Trust, State House Annex, Concord, New Hampshire 03301. $2.00. Annual supplement, which includes changes, deletions, and additions, available from the same address for $2.00.

New Jersey (321 foundations and 374 corporations). *The New Jersey Mitchell Guide: Foundations, Corporations, and Their Managers*. 2nd edition. Edited by Janet A. Mitchell. 1980. vi, 218 p. Based on 1977 and 1978 990-PF and 990-AR returns filed with the IRS and information supplied by foundations. Main section arranged alphabetically by foundation; entries include sample grants and officers; no statement of purpose. Also sections on corporations and scholarship foundations. Indexes of foundations and corporations by county and by managers. Listing of deletions from 1977 *Directory of New Jersey Foundations*. Appendixes of foundation statistics, foundations with assets over $1 million, and foundations with grant totals over $100,000. Available from The Mitchell Guides, P.O. Box 413, Princeton, New Jersey 08540. $20.00 prepaid.

New Mexico (approximately 41 foundations). *New Mexico Private Foundations Directory*. Edited by William G. Murrell, and William M. Miller. 1982. 77 p. Main section arranged alphabetically by foundation; entries include contact person, program purpose, areas of interest, financial data, application procedure, meeting times and publications. Also sections on proposal writing, private and corporate grantmanship and bibliography. No indexes. Available from New Moon Consultants, P.O. Box 532, Tijeras, New Mexico 87059. $5.50 plus $1.00 postage.

New York (approximately 139 organizations). *Guide to Grantmakers: Rochester Area*. Compiled by the Monroe County Library System. 1980. vii, 1030 p. Based on contact with organizations and 1977 through 1980 (mostly 1979) 990-PF and 990-AR returns filed with the IRS. Main section arranged alphabetically by organization, including foundations, corporations, associations, nonprofit organizations, and individuals offering funds, services, or products; entries include statement of purpose and officers; no sample grants. Also a section on liquidated and relocated foundations. Index of fields of interest. Appendixes of glossary of terms and bibliography. Published by Urban Information Center, Monroe County Library System. Not available for purchase. May be used in libraries of Monroe County Library System and at Foundation Center Library, New York.

New York (185 foundations, 182 businesses, and 42 parent corporations). *The Long Island Mitchell Guide: Foundations, Corporations, and Their Managers*. Edited by Janet A. Mitchell. 1980. vii, 119 p. Based on mostly 1978 and 1979 990-PF and 990-AR returns filed with the IRS by foundations on Long Island and in Brooklyn and Queens. Main section arranged alphabetically by foundation; entries include sample grants and officers; no statement of purpose. Also sections on businesses and their parent corporations. Indexes of foundations and corporations by name and by managers. Appendixes of foundation statistics, foundations with assets over $500,000, and foundations with grant totals over $50,000. Available from The Mitchell Guides, P.O. Box 413, Princeton, New Jersey 08540. $20.00 prepaid.

New York (323 foundations, 362 businesses, and 88 parent corporations). *The Upstate New York Mitchell Guide: Foundations, Corporations, and Their Managers*. Edited by Janet A. Mitchell. 1980. vii, 216 p. Based on mostly 1978 990-PF and 990-AR returns filed with the IRS by foundations in upstate New York and Westchester County. Main section ar-

135

ranged alphabetically by foundation; entries include sample grants and officers; no statement of purpose. Also sections on businesses and their parent corporations. Indexes of foundations and corporations by regions and by managers. Appendixes of foundation statistics, foundations with assets over $1 million, and foundations with grant totals over $10,000. Available from The Mitchell Guides, P.O. Box 413, Princeton, New Jersey 08540. $25.00 prepaid.

Ohio (1700 foundations). *Charitable Foundations Directory of Ohio*. 5th edition. 1982. 101 p. Based on 1977 through 1982 records in the Ohio Attorney General's Office and returns filed with the IRS. Main section arranged alphabetically by foundation; entries include statement of purpose and contact person; no sample grants. Indexes of foundations by county location and purpose. Available from Charitable Foundations Directory, Attorney General's Office, 30 East Broad Street, 15th Floor, Columbus, Ohio 43215. $5.00 prepaid.

Ohio (42 foundations). *Guide to Charitable Foundations in the Greater Akron Area*. 1st edition. Prepared by Human Services Planning Library. 1978. iii, 63 p. Based on United Way files, the Charitable Foundations Directory of Ohio, 990-PF and 990-AR returns filed with the IRS, and information supplied by foundations. Main section arranged alphabetically by foundation; entries include statement of purpose, sample grants, and officers. Also sections on scholarship foundations and proposal writing. Appendixes include list of recently terminated Akron area foundations; indexes of assets, grants, subject categories, and officers and trustees. Available from Human Services Planning Library, United Way of Summit County, P.O. Box 1260, 90 North Prospect Street, Akron, Ohio 44303. $2.50.

Oklahoma (approximately 150 foundations). *Directory of Oklahoma Foundations*. Edited by Thomas E. Broce. 1982. 284 p. Based on data from cooperating foundations or from 1974 through 1981 990-PF and 990-AR returns filed with the IRS. Main section arranged alphabetically by foundation; entries include statement of purpose and officers for some foundations; no sample grants. Index of foundation grant activities. Available from University of Oklahoma Press, 1005 Asp Avenue, Norman, Oklahoma 73069. $22.50 plus $.86 postage.

Oregon (approximately 430 foundations). *The Guide to Oregon Foundations*. 2nd edition. Produced by the Tri-County Community Council. 1981. xv, 208 p. Based on mostly 1979 and 1980 990-PF and 990-AR and CT-15 forms filed with the Oregon Register of Charitable Trusts and information supplied by foundations. Main section arranged alphabetically by foundation within six subdivisions: general purpose foundations, special purpose foundations, and national foundations with an active interest in Oregon; entries include statement of purpose, sample grants, and officers. Appendixes of advisory committee for *Guide*, Oregon foundations having assets of $500,00 or more, Oregon foundations making grants of $50,000 or more, terminated foundations, inactive foundations, new foundations, regional breakdown of foundations, national foundation grants to Oregon, Oregon community foundations, glossary of fundraising terms, and grants retrieval service. Index of foundation names. Available from Tri-County Community Council, 718 West Burnside, Portland, Oregon 97209. $10.00 plus $.50 postage.

Pennsylvania (2267 foundations). *Directory of Pennsylvania Foundations.* 2nd edition. Compiled by S. Damon Kletzien, editor, with assistance from Margaret H. Chalfant and Frances C. Ritchey. 1980. xv, 280 p. Based on 1979 and 1980 990-PF and 990-AR returns filed with the IRS and information supplied by foundations. Main section arranged alphabetically within geographic regions; entries include statement of purpose, sample grants, and officers for 914 foundations meeting criteria of assets exceeding $75,000 or awarding grants totaling $4,000 or more; for foundations under criteria, entries include foundation name and address only. Appendixes on approaching foundations, program planning and proposal writing, and broadening the foundation search. Indexes of officers, directors and trustees; major interests; and foundation names. Available from *Directory of Pennsylvania Foundations*, c/o Friends of the Free Library, Logan Square at 19th Street, Philadelphia, Pennsylvania 19103. Make check payable to: Friends of the Free Library of Philadelphia. $18.50 plus $1.11 for PA sales tax if applicable.

South Carolina (203 foundations). *South Carolina Foundation Directory.* 1st edition. Edited by Anne K. Middleton. 1978. 53 p. Based on 1975 990-PF and 990-AR returns filed with the IRS. Main section arranged alphabetically by foundation; entries include areas of interest and principal officer; no sample grants. Indexes of cities and fields of interest. Available from Anne K. Middleton, Assistant Reference Librarian, South Carolina State Library, P.O. Box 11469, Columbia, South Carolina 29211. Send $.70 in postage stamps.

Tennessee (202 foundations). See **Kentucky.**

Texas (approximately 1374 foundations). *Directory of Texas Foundations.* 6th edition. Compiled and edited by William J. Hooper, Jr. 1982. vi, 192 p. Based on mostly 1981 990-PF and 990-AR returns filed with the IRS. Main section arranged alphabetically by foundation; entries include areas of interest and contact person; no sample grants. Also a section on dissolved foundations. Indexes of areas of interest and cities. Available from Texas Foundations Research Center, P.O. Box 5494, Austin, Texas 78763. Make check payable to: TRFC. $26.50 prepaid. Add $1.00 for sales tax if applicable.

Texas (approximately 200 foundations). *The Guide to Texas Foundations.* 2nd edition. Edited by Jed Riffe. 1980. 103 p. Based on data from cooperating foundations and from 1977 and 1978 records in the Texas Attorney General's Office and Dallas Public Library. Main section arranged alphabetically by city location of foundation; entries include statement of purpose, sample grants, and officers. Covers foundations with grant totals over $30,000 per year. Indexes of foundation names and areas of interest. Available from Marianne Cline, Dallas Public Library, 1954 Commerce Street, Dallas, Texas 75201. $10.00 prepaid.

Virginia (approximately 390 foundations). *Virginia Foundations.* [1981] 130 p. Based on 1980 990-PF and 990-AR returns filed with the IRS. Main section arranged alphabetically by foundation; entries include statement of purpose and principal officer; no sample grants. Index of foundation names. Published by the Grants Resources Library of Hampton, Virginia; not available for sale. May be used in Foundation Center cooperating collections in Virginia and at Foundation Center libraries in New York and Washington, D.C.

Virginia (326 foundations). See **Kentucky.**

Washington (approximately 968 organizations). *Charitable Trust Directory.* 2nd edition. Compiled by the Office of the Attorney General. 1980. 242 p. Based on 1979 records in the Washington Attorney General's Office. Includes information on all charitable organizations and trusts reporting to Attorney General under the Washington Charitable Trust Act. Main section arranged alphabetically by organization; entries include statement of purpose and officers. No sample grants or indexes. Available from the Office of the Attorney General, Temple of Justice, Olympia, Washington 98504. $4.00 prepaid.

West Virginia (approximately 99 foundations). *West Virginia Foundation Directory.* Compiled and edited by William Seeto. 1979. 49 p. Based on 1977 and 1978 990-PF and 990-AR returns filed with the IRS. Main section arranged alphabetically by foundation; entries include sample grants, and officers; no statement of purpose. Also a section on inactive or terminated foundations. Index of counties and cities. Available from West Virginia Foundation Directory, Box 96, Route 1, Terra Alta, West Virginia 26764. Make check payable to: West Virginia Foundation Directory. $7.95 prepaid.

Wisconsin (643 foundations). *Foundations in Wisconsin: A Directory 1980.* 6th edition. Compiled by Susan S. Hopwood. 1982. xiii 280 p. Based on 1980 and 1981 990-PF and 990-AR returns filed with the IRS. Main section arranged alphabetically by foundation; entries include areas of interest and officers; no sample grants. Also sections listing inactive foundations, terminated foundations, and operating foundations. Indexes of areas of interest, counties, and foundation managers. Available from

The Foundation Collection, Marquette University Memorial Library, 1415 West Wisconsin Avenue, Milwaukee, Wisconsin 53233. $15.00 prepaid plus $.75 sales tax for Wisconsin residents, or Wisconsin tax exempt number.

Wyoming (45 foundations). *Wyoming Foundations Directory*. Prepared by Joy Riske. 1982. 2nd edtion. 54 p. Based on 1980 through 1982 990-PF and 990-AR returns filed with the IRS and a survey of the foundations. Main section arranged alphabetically by foundation; entries include statement of purpose and contact person when available. Also sections on foundations based out-of-state that award grants to Wyoming and a list of foundations awarding educational loans and scholarships. Index of foundations. Available from Laramie County Community College Library, 1400 East College Drive, Cheyenne, Wyoming 82001. Free. $1.00 postage for out of state orders.

Wyoming (12 foundations). See **Montana.**